T0361705

The Declutter DEVOTIONAL

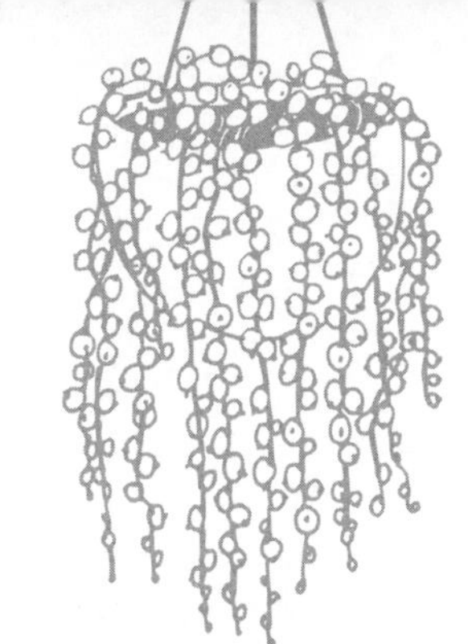

The Declutter DEVOTIONAL

Biblical Inspiration
for Making Room for
What Matters

CAREY SCOTT

BARBOUR
PUBLISHING

Print ISBN 979-8-89151-050-0

Published by Barbour Publishing, Inc., 1810 Barbour Drive, Uhrichsville, Ohio 44683, www.barbourbooks.com

Our mission is to inspire the world with the life-changing message of the Bible.

Printed in China.

"Stop storing up treasures
for yourselves on earth,
where moths and rust destroy
and thieves break in and steal.
Instead, store up treasures
for yourselves in heaven,
where moths and rust
don't destroy and thieves
don't break in and steal.
*Your heart will be
where your treasure is."*

MATTHEW 6:19-21 GW

INTRODUCTION

This world has a way of cluttering our hearts with all the wrong things. We are bombarded daily by earthly remedies that offer little or no lasting relief for the believer. And rather than bring hope to our weary spirit, they often litter our life with broken promises and unmet expectations. In our human condition, it's not hard to fall prey to things like doubt, worry, fear, and insecurities. But that's not the way God wants us to live.

Instead, the Lord longs for us to purge those unhealthy habits and fill the empty spaces with a robust belief in His goodness and provision. It's through a relationship with the Lord that we're able to stand in the freedom Christ came to give. We don't have to live encumbered by every challenging circumstance and strenuous struggle. As we trust God each step of the way, we will experience a heart uncluttered by life and full of faith.

Each devotion in this book is designed to remind you of God's promises of help and hope to those who seek Him. You are seen. You are known. You are loved. And your God is with you always. Let Him speak through these pages and spark a greater awareness of what fills your heart—be it earthly clutter or the eternal Christ. Let Him lead you into a life of liberty!

THE PROPER ORDER

Just maintain the proper order in all things.
1 CORINTHIANS 14:40 VOICE

While this passage from 1 Corinthians talks specifically about prophecy and praying in the Spirit, the wisdom in this verse can be applied to other areas of life. It's important to remember that we serve a God who values order. From the creation story to the way He knit you together in your mother's womb, His thoughtful design and careful craftsmanship are on display. And because we live in a chaotic world, full of disorder and discouragement, choosing to "maintain the proper order" will help keep our hearts at peace.

How do we walk this out in our day-to-day life? Consider that maybe, just maybe, taking one step at a time is prudent. The best way forward might be choosing to focus on the next right step rather than allowing our mind to be cluttered with every single detail. Too often, we look way down the road, which leaves us overwhelmed by everything that needs to be done. We feel scared and stressed. And instead of seeing good things ahead, we imagine horrible outcomes and endings.

But, friend, God is a God of order. He fully understands your situation. He has complete clarity. So why not invite Him into the process of taking one step at a time, asking for guidance and wisdom? Let God help you "maintain the proper order in all things."

Dear Lord, I confess I try to figure things out on my own. I need Your help to know what to do next. In Jesus' name, amen.

LETTING PEACE PREVAIL

God is not a God of disorder but a God of peace.

1 CORINTHIANS 14:33 GW

If you let it, today's verse will help to settle your anxious heart. It will remind you that God is in control, without fail. It will bring a sense of calm into your chaotic day. But it requires you to grab hold of this beautiful truth and give your day to Him through prayer.

As women, we regularly pile too much on our plate of responsibility. Our to-do list becomes a novel-length inventory of chores that no mere mortal can complete in a day. And we're guilty of filling our schedule to the brim in an effort to keep up. No wonder we battle anxiety and worry! We wake each morning already set up for failure.

But knowing that God operates through order is a blessing for us! It means we start our day in prayer, asking *Him* to order our steps correctly. We let *Him* prioritize what matters most, even if some things don't make the day's list. We adopt *His* pace and cadence rather than rush around in a frenzy. And as we let God lead our waking hours, peace will prevail.

Dear Lord, I'm tired of filling my days my way because it leaves me exhausted and overwhelmed. Help me to recognize what matters most and guide my steps so I live in joy and peace. In Jesus' name, amen.

LIFE IS FULL OF SEASONS

A time to start looking and a time to stop looking, a time to keep and a time to throw away, a time to tear apart and a time to sew together, a time to keep quiet and a time to speak out.

ECCLESIASTES 3:6–7 GW

Life is full of seasons. Today's verses confirm that truth with precision. The takeaway is knowing that there is a time for everything, and this truth can be comforting when we're struggling.

When our mind is inundated with financial challenges, or when we're in a messy moment in our marriage, or when parenting feels engulfing, or when our career requires too much of us, we can exhale because we know this is a season. And what's more, it shall pass. Our current situation isn't our forever situation.

That holds true when the storms of life are at bay too. When you're in a sweet spot in your important relationships, and your income is steady, and work brings joy, and the kids are behaving, it's also a season. What remains constant is the goodness of God.

Friend, you can breathe in His goodness regardless of the changing seasons. When you do, the Lord will declutter your heart and mind of doom and gloom, freeing you to focus on His faithfulness instead. Life changes, but God never does.

Dear Lord, thank You for the reminder that life is full of seasons, but You are evergreen. In Jesus' name, amen.

WORKING SMARTER AND WITH PURPOSE

Work hard so God can say to you, "Well done." Be a good workman, one who does not need to be ashamed when God examines your work. Know what his Word says and means.

2 TIMOTHY 2:15 TLB

Working hard doesn't mean wearing yourself out. The Lord isn't asking you to fill your days, nights, and weekends to the point of exhaustion. His plan for your life doesn't include being constantly tuckered out and worn down. Consider that maybe God is asking you to work smarter and with purpose.

Whether it's in an office or at home, we have work to accomplish each day. From meal planning to carpooling to preparing a report, we're to work hard. And when we do so with the intention of pleasing God, we'll find the supernatural strength we need to do our best.

Before you get out of bed in the morning, ask the Lord to strengthen you for the day ahead. Ask for help to complete each task with a faithful heart set on pleasing Him. Rather than piling it on, watch and listen for Him to set the pace and order your steps. And ask for a peaceful spirit, unencumbered by bitterness or stress.

Dear Lord, help me to work smarter and with purpose so that in the end, You'll say, "Well done." I want to please You. Show me how to declutter unrealistic expectations and embrace Your plan for my day. In Jesus' name, amen.

WHERE IS YOUR TREASURE?

Then Jesus said to them, "Watch out! Guard yourself against all kinds of greed. After all, one's life isn't determined by one's possessions, even when someone is very wealthy."

LUKE 12:15 CEB

Take those words in, friend. Let them lighten your load today. And meditate on this powerful truth: *Life isn't determined by one's possessions.* Honestly, this flies in the face of what the world preaches. Its message is the exact opposite, telling us from an early age that the one with the most toys wins. Because of that, far too many of us have gone to great lengths to partner with this destructive lie. Our homes are cluttered with proof.

Greed doesn't glorify God. Instead, it glorifies self. We collect things to fill an empty space in our hearts that only the Lord Himself can fill. We accumulate stuff to feel better, but it fails in the end. Matthew 6:21 (VOICE) says, "For where your treasure is, there your heart will be also." So, friend, is your treasure stockpiled here or stored up in heaven?

Let's not fill our homes with earthly goodies, because they cannot calm a heart, settle a spirit, or usher in peace—at least not for long. Instead, let's litter our life with signs that our faith in God is strong and unshakable.

Dear Lord, I confess that I've looked to the world for satisfaction. I've collected earthly treasures trying to find what only You can offer. Today, I choose to get rid of greed. In Jesus' name, amen.

WORTHLESS EARTHLY TREASURES

Some people store up treasures in their homes here on earth. This is a shortsighted practice—don't undertake it. Moths and rust will eat up any treasure you may store here. Thieves may break into your homes and steal your precious trinkets. Instead, put up your treasures in heaven where moths do not attack, where rust does not corrode, and where thieves are barred at the door.

MATTHEW 6:19–20 VOICE

Today's passage is crystal clear to believers, telling us we have a choice to make. This choice may seem like a no-brainer, but it's harder than you think. It takes intentionality to do the right thing. It takes confidence to make hard choices. It takes faith to live with a divine perspective. That's why we need God's wisdom and discernment to guide our steps.

There is nothing wrong with wearing cute clothes or decorating your home. We can drive nice cars and go on vacation. But Jesus' words are weighty. They're a timely warning to take inventory of our hearts—our motives. Are we more focused on collecting worldly things than on living in ways that glorify God? Is our desire to keep up with others or to invest in our relationship with the Lord?

If we're not steeped in prayer and encouraged by the Word every day, our eyes will quickly turn from God to focus on new and shiny things around us.

Dear Lord, help me to declutter my heart of worthless earthly treasures. In Jesus' name, amen.

LIES OF WORTHLESSNESS

"Aren't five sparrows sold for two cents? God doesn't forget any of them. Even every hair on your head has been counted. Don't be afraid! You are worth more than many sparrows."

LUKE 12:6–7 GW

Sometimes we fill our brain with lies of worthlessness. We entertain the idea that we're not good enough to be loved. That no matter how hard we try to be of value, we simply are not. And we end up questioning the very foundation of who we are. And at the same time, we question God's ability to create something wonderful.

Friend, have you been told by a parent or a significant other that you don't measure up? Maybe you've failed a few times, causing you to feel unimportant. Or maybe when you compare yourself to others, you fall flat. . .at least in your opinion. Respectfully, it's time to rewrite that narrative. It's time to clear out the lies weighing you down.

The Bible says you matter so much to God that He knows the number of hairs on your head. He knows how many you started out the day with and how many fell out by bedtime. In His great love, He cares about the smallest details concerning you. Ask the Lord to fill your heart with truth!

Dear Lord, I've allowed the lies of worthlessness into my heart, and they've caused chaos. Please remove them so I can stand in the freedom of who I am in You! In Jesus' name, amen.

CHOKING YOUR FAITH

But the things of this life—the worries, the drive for more and more, the desire for other things—those things cluster around close and choke the life of God out of them until they cannot produce.

MARK 4:19 VOICE

Today's verse paints a vivid word picture of warning. And for believers, there's a great benefit to understanding this reality, because there truly are *things* that cluster close and choke our faith.

When we stress over situations and relationships, or let greed push us toward wanting the latest and greatest, or live in a state of discontentment with what we have, joy gets choked out. We're left feeling disgruntled and lamenting our perceived lack. Our hearts get cluttered with worldly woes, while our faith—our ability to trust God—gets shoved aside. And we're rendered ineffective as disciples because our lives preach the wrong message.

The Lord is with you, friend. He sees all the things strangling your ability to rest in Him. Ask God to help you release the earthly distresses and set your sights on the eternal delights. Ask for hope, joy, and peace! And ask Him to free you from everything choking your faith today.

Dear Lord, I know Your plan is for me to live in the fullness of my faith. May I cling to You, trusting Your hand to free me from all that hinders. In Jesus' name, amen.

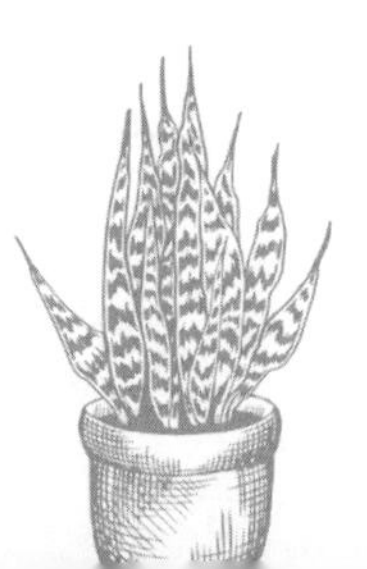

THE TENDENCY TOWARD SELFISHNESS

Then he told them a parable: "A certain rich man's land produced a bountiful crop. He said to himself, What will I do? I have no place to store my harvest! Then he thought, Here's what I'll do. I'll tear down my barns and build bigger ones. That's where I'll store all my grain and goods. I'll say to myself, You have stored up plenty of goods, enough for several years. Take it easy! Eat, drink, and enjoy yourself."

LUKE 12:16–19 CEB

This section of scripture in the book of Luke is referred to as the parable of the rich fool because this man went to great lengths to care for his earthly needs. He had enough to help others—to fulfill his moral responsibility—but instead, he hoarded it all for himself.

The problem wasn't the bountiful crop or the wealth it provided. The problem was that he coveted it. He became self-seeking. And he fell into complacency. He squashed God's blessing with selfishness.

Let's be careful that we don't follow suit. Let's approach life with our hands open and our palms facing up. Every good thing comes from the Lord, and we're to be generous with each blessing. Hoarding good things for ourselves merely exposes a lack of trust that He will meet every need, every time.

Dear Lord, thank You for trusting me with blessings. Help me to steward them in ways that glorify You. In Jesus' name, amen.

WHERE IS YOUR HEART'S FOCUS?

No one can serve two masters. If you try, you will wind up loving the first master and hating the second, or vice versa. People try to serve both God and money—but you can't. You must choose one or the other.

MATTHEW 6:24 VOICE

Every day, we have a choice to make about where we focus our hearts. We must decide whom we will serve—God or money. The former ushers in freedom and peace, while the latter keeps our hearts in bondage, manifesting as obsession or a constant striving for more. Money as master keeps accounts of where we're deficient and encourages us to desire earthly treasures above all else.

But that's not the Lord's plan for those who love Him. Instead, He wants us to experience the liberation provided by Jesus' death on the cross. If we embrace His will above our own wants and serve God with our choices, we will.

Friend, this isn't always easy to do! The heart wants what the heart wants. And our only hope of living with the right motivation is to stay connected to our source of strength. Time in the Word and in prayer will allow for a heart that's free from the world's clutter.

Dear Lord, deciding where to focus my heart is a daily battle. Too often I'm pulled in the wrong direction. Strengthen me to keep my eyes trained on You so the things of this world grow strangely dim. In Jesus' name, amen.

STOP WORRYING

"Don't chase after what you will eat and what you will drink. Stop worrying. All the nations of the world long for these things. Your Father knows that you need them. Instead, desire his kingdom and these things will be given to you as well."

LUKE 12:29–31 CEB

As women, we battle worry on so many fronts. Can we share a collective *amen*? Maybe more than men, we let fear crowd our faith and push out peace. And it feels like a heavy weight that keeps us from delighting in God's goodness.

What are you worrying about today, friend? Are you afraid you'll never find a husband or that your marriage is on the rocks? Is parenting a teenager stressing you out? Has an unexpected diagnosis left you anxious and unable to find your footing? Are you feeling doom and gloom about the economy or the state of the world? Honestly, there are a million things to worry about and one God who is sovereign over them all. We can trust them *all* to His care.

Let the Lord bring order to your turbulent heart by talking to Him about your struggles. Be honest about your fears and worries. God is present. He understands. And He knows exactly what you need.

Dear Lord, I confess my sin of worry! Please help me to rest in You, knowing You're in control and I am safe and loved! In Jesus' name, amen.

CHOOSING UNSELFISHNESS

"When you give to the poor, don't let your left hand know what your right hand is doing. Give your contributions privately. Your Father sees what you do in private. He will reward you."

MATTHEW 6:3–4 GW

Sometimes we fill up on ourselves and the good deeds we do. Rather than extending generosity with a level of privacy, we long to be seen. We want to be acknowledged because it makes us feel important. We want to be known as selfless. And while we may truly care about others, sometimes our main motive for helping is instinctively egocentric. This grieves God's heart.

Countless times throughout the Word, we're instructed to have a servant's attitude. We're to love others with kindness and generosity. But it's easy to let greed clutter our hearts and motivate us in all the wrong ways. Living altruistically is a daily choice, and God enables us to do so—it's being His hands and feet in the world.

Spend time today talking to the Lord and taking inventory of your motives. Confess the moments you've stepped out with a self-seeking attitude. Remember, there is no condemnation for the believer! We are free from it! But at the same time, there is always room to unpack the unwanted and start afresh.

Dear Lord, I am wretched without You. But when I lean in for guidance and direction, I'm able to walk in righteous ways that glorify Your name. In Jesus' name, amen.

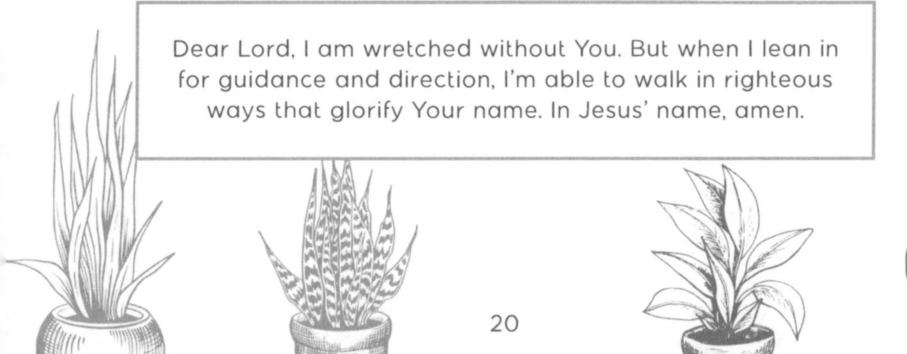

WHERE ARE YOU COLLECTING?

"Sell your material possessions, and give the money to the poor. Make yourselves wallets that don't wear out! Make a treasure for yourselves in heaven that never loses its value! In heaven thieves and moths can't get close enough to destroy your treasure. Your heart will be where your treasure is."

LUKE 12:33–34 GW

Is it time to declutter your home? Have you been in collector mode, falling prey to the world's offerings? Have you been caught up in keeping up? Maybe you've lost focus on where to store up treasures and you need a reboot in righteous living. Friend, sometimes it's easy to lose perspective. It's just an unfortunate part of the human condition.

Scripture says that where we work to collect—on earth or in heaven—is where our hearts lie too. Consider these questions with honesty: Has there been distance in your relationship with God? Has time in the Word or in prayer slid down the to-do list? Have you been more focused on your desires than those of the divine? Wherever we're determined to store up treasures reveals our deepest priorities.

Let today be a new start, a pivot back to what matters most. Confess and repent as you turn your eyes to God. And let Him give you an eternal perspective that helps you navigate life with purpose and passion.

Dear Lord, I want to store up my treasures in heaven. Please show me how. In Jesus' name, amen.

TRACK RECORD OF FAITHFULNESS

"Who among you by worrying can add a single moment to your life? If you can't do such a small thing, why worry about the rest? Notice how the lilies grow. They don't wear themselves out with work, and they don't spin cloth. But I say to you that even Solomon in all his splendor wasn't dressed like one of these."

LUKE 12:25–27 CEB

Have you noticed how easy it is to worry and how challenging it can be to trust God? Worrying feels like our default setting, and we sometimes wear it as a badge of honor. We may think it makes us look like a concerned mom who deeply loves her children. Or a committed wife, anxious over her husband's career. Or a responsible woman who's just trying to make ends meet. But the Bible clearly tells us that worry is worthless. It does nothing to help.

God doesn't want our hearts to be cluttered with anxious thoughts. Instead, our hearts should be full of faith. We're told to lay down our fears and trust that He is at work in every situation we face. It may feel counterintuitive, but God's ways are not our ways. And as we surrender our worry into His capable hands, we'll begin to see His perfect track record of faithfulness emerge.

Dear Lord, today I'm giving You all my worry because I know You're in control and working all things out! In Jesus' name, amen.

FOLLOWING GOD'S PLAN

Since we have such a huge crowd of men of faith watching us from the grandstands, let us strip off anything that slows us down or holds us back, and especially those sins that wrap themselves so tightly around our feet and trip us up; and let us run with patience the particular race that God has set before us.

HEBREWS 12:1 TLB

Friend, what are the things that have slowed you down and held you back from following God's plan for your life? What sins have wrapped themselves tightly around you, tripping you up so you stay ineffective or uninterested as a believer?

There are countless ways we can clutter our lives with everything but God's will. We can make a mess because of bad choices and overthinking. We can bring chaos and disorder by kicking the can down the road rather than confronting an issue head-on. And we can litter our lives with addiction, indiscretion, and indecision. All of these will cause us to stall.

But when we free ourselves by following God's plan—spending time in prayer and in the Word regularly—we will be empowered through faith to finish the race He's set before us. And heaven will cheer us on!

Dear Lord, I confess the times I've allowed sin to keep me from faithfully following You. Help me to stay free from its trap so nothing hinders me from running my race with purpose. In Jesus' name, amen.

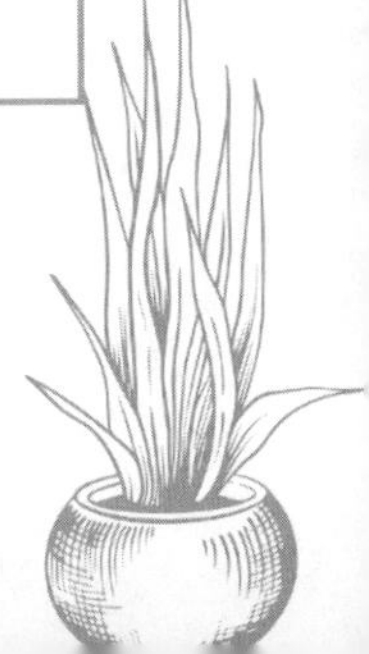

YOUR NEEDS MATTER TO GOD

Know this: my God will also fill every need you have according to His glorious riches in Jesus the Anointed, our Liberating King. So may our God and Father be glorified forever and ever. Amen.

PHILIPPIANS 4:19–20 VOICE

Sometimes we scramble to meet our needs. Rather than going directly to God, we work in our own strength, stirring up stress and strife along the way. Maybe we forget that He is our ultimate source. Maybe we think our need is too insignificant to involve Him. Maybe we feel more than capable of handling it ourselves. Or maybe, in the turmoil, we fail to remember that He's always there for us. Regardless of the reason, we eventually feel the squeeze of our human limitations.

Through his words in today's scripture, Paul wants us to *know* something very important. He reminds us that just as God has met his every need, He will do the same for us. It may not always be in the ways we want, but our needs matter to the Lord. He sees them. He knows them. And He will meet them.

What this means for you is that there's a powerful promise you can rest on. You can get off the treadmill of performance. You can break free from the idea that you must save yourself. You can push out the lies of self-sufficiency cluttering your heart and mind.

Dear Lord, I trust You to meet my every need. In Jesus' name, amen.

LIVING FAITHFULLY TODAY

So do not worry about tomorrow. Let tomorrow worry about itself. Living faithfully is a large enough task for today.
MATTHEW 6:34 VOICE

This verse from the book of Matthew reminds us to be present today rather than forecasting worries for tomorrow and letting them weigh us down. And if we're honest, many of us would admit that this is a big task because worry plays a robust role in our waking hours. It's constantly coursing through our veins and crowding our minds with anxious thoughts. So just how are we to live faithfully in the now?

This pursuit takes great intentionality on the part of a believer. It requires us to be aware when fear sneaks in and deal with it immediately. We can't let it fester. We can't allow it to choke out our peace. We can't entertain it, even for a second. Instead, we go straight to God in prayer and confess it. Because we're assured that He will listen, we talk to the Lord about every detail surrounding the worry. We get it all out. And then we ask for a greater measure of faith and step right back into our day, victorious.

Worrying about tomorrow fixes nothing and only robs us of joy. As believers, we never have to settle for this unhealthy pattern. We can choose to live faithfully today and trust that God already has tomorrow figured out.

Dear Lord, I'm trading my fear for faith. In Jesus' name, amen.

THE JOY AHEAD

We must focus on Jesus, the source and goal of our faith. He saw the joy ahead of him, so he endured death on the cross and ignored the disgrace it brought him. Now he holds the honored position—the one next to God the Father on the heavenly throne.

HEBREWS 12:2 GW

In today's scripture, did you notice what kept Jesus on the cross to endure unspeakable pain? Did you see what allowed Him to disregard the shame this kind of death was meant to produce? The writer of Hebrews said it was because Jesus "saw the joy ahead." Rather than sit in the mess of that moment, He was strengthened by what was coming.

Friend, Jesus' example is applicable to our lives right now. We can be inspired by this same powerful concept. By faith, we can keep our eyes trained on the eternal promises of God rather than letting the troubles of today hem us in. It doesn't minimize the magnitude of what we're facing, like marital sufferings, parenting struggles, financial worries, work cares, or health problems. It simply allows our hearts to rest in the joy ahead. It strengthens us to stand strong, knowing these current difficulties are seasonal.

Let's remember to focus on Jesus, who is—and always will be—the source and goal of our faith. In Him, we can endure to the end.

Dear Lord, in all things, help me to focus on the joy ahead. In Jesus' name, amen.

REJOICE ALWAYS

Most of all, friends, always rejoice in the Lord! I never tire of saying it: Rejoice! Keep your gentle nature so that all people will know what it looks like to walk in His footsteps. The Lord is ever present with us.

PHILIPPIANS 4:4–5 VOICE

Paul's directive is crystal clear for believers. We are to rejoice in the Lord *always*. He is instructing us to walk this out every day, even when we don't feel like it. If we're struggling with our faith, we're to rejoice regardless. And just how are we to do this?

Rather than clutter our minds with all that's challenging or going wrong, we're instead to consider the ways in which God works. We may be sad, angry, hurt, grieving, hungry, or tired, but we can still find the gumption to rejoice in the Lord.

In every moment, let's choose to give thanks because we know He is working in our situation. Let's remember His perfect track record in our lives. Let's rest knowing He'll meet our every need, at the right time and in the right way. Let's exhale, knowing that the perfect will of God will be done. And let's spend time in the Word, being reminded that He will provide, save, heal, restore, and guide.

Even more, let's choose to rejoice always, since doing so ushers in a powerful peace as we wait for the Lord to answer our prayers.

Dear Lord, remind me to rejoice in You always! In Jesus' name, amen.

FREED UP THROUGH FAITH

Not that I was ever in need, for I have learned how to get along happily whether I have much or little. I know how to live on almost nothing or with everything. I have learned the secret of contentment in every situation, whether it be a full stomach or hunger, plenty or want; for I can do everything God asks me to with the help of Christ who gives me the strength and power.

PHILIPPIANS 4:11–13 TLB

Just like Paul, we too can learn to be content in every situation when we ask for help from the Lord. He is the one who will strengthen us with an eternal perspective and help us to resist the worldly persuasions to be hyperfocused on ourselves.

Of course, our needs are important. Some things are necessary for our survival and our ability to walk out our God-designed calling. But don't think for one moment that your Father isn't keenly aware of those needs. The key here is trusting God and His timing so that your current lack doesn't fill you with worry.

We can't be others-focused when we're self-focused. And when we lean on the Lord and believe His provision will be perfectly timed, we are freed up through faith. His strength and power are what fuel us forward. So, friend, never doubt that you can do all God asks with His help.

Dear Lord, remove everything earthly that keeps me from seeing everything eternally. In Jesus' name, amen.

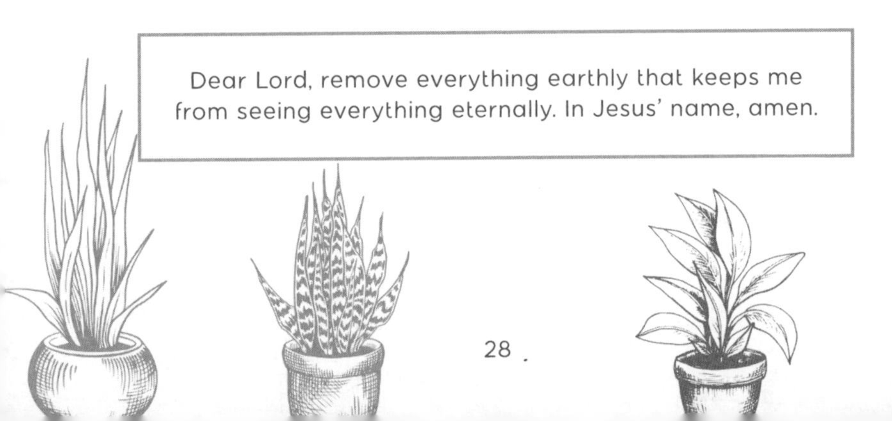

THINK ABOUT JESUS

Consider the life of the One who endured such personal attacks and hostility from sinners so that you will not grow weary or lose heart. Among you, in your striving against sin, none has resisted the pressure to the point of death, as He did.

HEBREWS 12:3–4 VOICE

When the struggles we're facing make us feel like the walls are closing in on us, we're told to think about Jesus. Remember all He endured while on His earthly mission to bridge the gap that sin created between us and God. And when we consider His sufferings and the way He held on patiently and with great purpose, His example emboldens us to stand strong as well.

When your child is acting out rebelliously or you're struggling to get pregnant, hold on. When your desire to get married seems hopeless or your marriage is careening toward divorce, don't give up. When you're headed toward bankruptcy, or seem to be losing a health battle, or are reeling from a friend's betrayal, stay in the fight. Let Jesus' example strengthen you. And don't forget that while He was fully God, He was also fully man as He endured earthly hostility. There was no divine superpower at play.

So don't allow the challenges you're facing to litter your heart with discouragement. Don't let them push out your faith. Jesus' ability to endure should be what encourages us every day!

Dear Lord, thank You for the life of Jesus!
In Jesus' name, amen.

LETTING GO OF THE PAST

It's not that I have already reached this goal or have already been perfected, but I pursue it, so that I may grab hold of it because Christ grabbed hold of me for just this purpose. Brothers and sisters, I myself don't think I've reached it, but I do this one thing: I forget about the things behind me and reach out for the things ahead of me. The goal I pursue is the prize of God's upward call in Christ Jesus.

PHILIPPIANS 3:12–14 CEB

Lucky for us, perfection is not the goal of our lives—at least not in the eyes of God. Until we see Jesus face-to-face, the reality is that we will struggle. We live in a fallen world where sin is a daily challenge for us all. We will flounder and fail. We will disappoint God, ourselves, and others. Even the apostle Paul saw the effects of his humanity. But that doesn't mean we give up pursuing the purpose the Lord has for us.

Instead, Paul shares insights that we can grab on to today. He tells us that he lets go of the past and pushes forward. He declutters his mind and heart from the failures of yesterday and, in faith, reaches out for what's to come tomorrow. Maybe it's time for you to do the same.

Dear Lord, help me to let go of the times I've messed up and pursue with passion Your perfect plan for my life. In Jesus' name, amen.

WORLDLY THINGS

In the end they will be destroyed. Their own emotions are their god, and they take pride in the shameful things they do. Their minds are set on worldly things. We, however, are citizens of heaven. We look forward to the Lord Jesus Christ coming from heaven as our Savior. Through his power to bring everything under his authority, he will change our humble bodies and make them like his glorified body.

PHILIPPIANS 3:19–21 GW

Let's be careful not to set our minds on worldly things. Let's not allow our homes and hearts to be cluttered with earthly treasures. When we give our feelings permission to rule the day, we're putting them above God. When we're proud or unconcerned about walking in our fleshly desires, it's an offense against the Lord. As believers our citizenship is in heaven, and that mindset should govern how we live right now.

So let's choose to be unchained to the world's ways. By faith, we are free! Let's keep our eyes on Him as we navigate each day, working for His glory while waiting for His return. If we collect anything, let's collect scripture in our hearts. Let's gather others for the kingdom. And let's rejoice that our lives are littered with His goodness, proving the Lord's unshakable faithfulness to those who love Him.

Dear Lord, help me to keep my mind set on eternal things rather than earthly ones. In Jesus' name, amen.

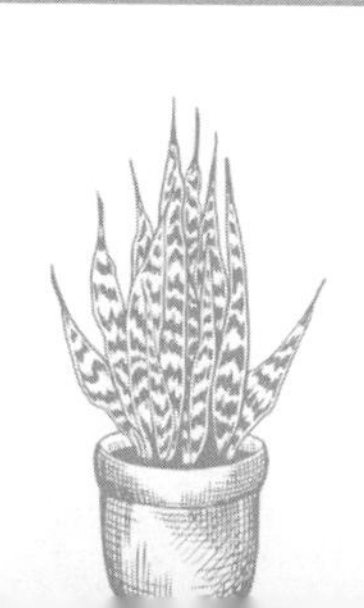

NEVER WORRY

Never worry about anything. But in every situation let God know what you need in prayers and requests while giving thanks. Then God's peace, which goes beyond anything we can imagine, will guard your thoughts and emotions through Christ Jesus.

PHILIPPIANS 4:6–7 GW

Based on today's scripture, when is it okay for us to worry? Is it only when relationships are hard or when we're strapped financially? Can we worry about our prodigal child or the health of aging parents? How about the state of the world? Can we let fear overtake us regarding current events? Can we worry about school or our career, knowing how challenging they can be at times? Can our heart be anxious about the future and what it may bring? For believers, the answer is simple: no.

Paul clearly states that we are *never* to worry about anything. Instead of allowing fear to clutter our thoughts, we're instructed to pray. As a matter of fact, he directs us to pray in *every* situation! We're to tell God each burden, let Him know what we need, and thank Him in advance because we believe He's faithful. And when we do, an unexplainable peace will push out the worry and we'll find rest in the Lord.

Remember that worry gets us nowhere good. It fixes nothing. But prayer does, and we can talk to God about anything at any time.

Dear Lord, help me to kick my worrying habit to the curb by praying instead. In Jesus' name, amen.

A CHANGE IN PRIORITIES

But all these things that I once thought very worthwhile—now I've thrown them all away so that I can put my trust and hope in Christ alone. Yes, everything else is worthless when compared with the priceless gain of knowing Christ Jesus my Lord. I have put aside all else, counting it worth less than nothing, in order that I can have Christ.

PHILIPPIANS 3:7–8 TLB

Paul's priorities changed, and things that were once seen as worthwhile in his eyes—like power and notoriety—became worthless to him. What he now considered invaluable was knowing Jesus. Everything that once meant so much was downgraded. Paul's faith reworked his focus. And his relationship with God removed the worldly (and religious) goals that had littered his heart.

What a powerful demonstration of how God changes us from the inside out! As believers, we should want to know Him more than anything else. This shift in priorities doesn't downplay the fact that we have things to do here—divine plans He created for us. We are called to love and serve others with purpose. But it does remind us that our allegiance should be first and foremost to God. . .and from there, we should prioritize our days.

Ask the Lord to reveal any misplaced loyalties or pursuits in your life. Ask for insights into any upside-down or backward thinking. Knowing Him should be the only thing that crowds your heart.

Dear Lord, knowing You is priceless!
In Jesus' name, amen.

EMBRACING GODLY DISCIPLINE

For a short time our fathers disciplined us as they thought best. Yet, God disciplines us for our own good so that we can become holy like him. We don't enjoy being disciplined. It always seems to cause more pain than joy. But later on, those who learn from that discipline have peace that comes from doing what is right.

HEBREWS 12:10–11 GW

The writer of Hebrews is spot-on. As adults, we don't enjoy being called out by others. We don't like getting in trouble for what we do or what we say. It's not that we don't want opportunities to improve ourselves or be encouraged to make better choices. . .it's that we don't want someone else to point out where we're falling short. Amen?

But when the correction comes from the Lord, we can be assured it's done in love and with the right motives. We can trust that the timing is perfect. We can accept it because it's not given in condemnation. So while we may struggle to accept worldly reproach, it's always in our best interest to embrace godly discipline.

Just like any good and loving father, the Lord wants the very best for His daughters. And like any good and loving daughter, we should desire to do the Father's will. Let's keep our hearts freed up so we can clearly hear God's direction and discipline.

> Dear Lord, help me to embrace Your discipline, knowing it's loving and perfect. In Jesus' name, amen.

WE DON'T HAVE TO FIGURE IT ALL OUT

"He lifts the poor from the dust—yes, from a pile of ashes—and treats them as princes sitting in the seats of honor. For all the earth is the Lord's and he has set the world in order."

1 SAMUEL 2:8 TLB

This passage from 1 Samuel is part of Hannah's prayer. She struggled to get pregnant and took her broken heart to God, asking for His intervention. And in her petitions, she promised to dedicate her child back to the Lord for all his days. This prayer starts with Hannah sharing very personal emotions and ends with her recognizing God's sovereignty and ability to uphold the order of the earth.

Maybe you can relate to Hannah's gratitude, knowing that at the end of the day, God holds the whole world in His loving and capable hands. It's not our job to figure everything out. Instead, we can share our burdens with God and release them. We can trust that He's working all things for our good and His glory, in His perfect timing. And when we're burned out and broken, we can know with certainty that God will pull us from the ashes and bring restoration.

Friend, what is the Holy Spirit speaking to you right now? What encouragement is He bringing to your weary heart? Where are you feeling seen or heard by the Lord today?

Dear Lord, I know You are in control, and I'm grateful. In Jesus' name, amen.

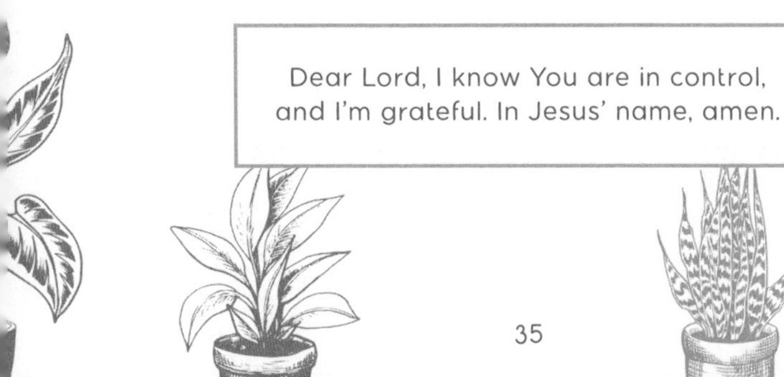

FILLING YOUR HEART WITH GOOD THINGS

Summing it all up, friends, I'd say you'll do best by filling your minds and meditating on things true, noble, reputable, authentic, compelling, gracious—the best, not the worst; the beautiful, not the ugly; things to praise, not things to curse. Put into practice what you learned from me, what you heard and saw and realized. Do that, and God, who makes everything work together, will work you into his most excellent harmonies.

PHILIPPIANS 4:8–9 MSG

What if you made a conscious decision to declutter your mind from worldly woes and instead fill it with things listed in today's scripture? What if you were an active gatekeeper, tossing out stinkin' thinkin' anytime it worked its way in? Since we know that what's in our minds—in our hearts—usually informs our words and actions, being attentive makes good sense.

Faith is active and requires our daily participation to grow. But if we entertain negative and ugly thoughts, allowing them to take root, they will begin to choke out our faith. We won't easily see the beautiful and best. We won't consider what's praiseworthy and positive. Instead, we'll focus on things that dampen our belief in God's goodness.

Let's heed Paul's wise directive and watch what we allow our minds to meditate on.

Dear Lord, there are times when my mind wanders in all the wrong directions. Help me to be active in choosing what I allow myself to meditate on. In Jesus' name, amen.

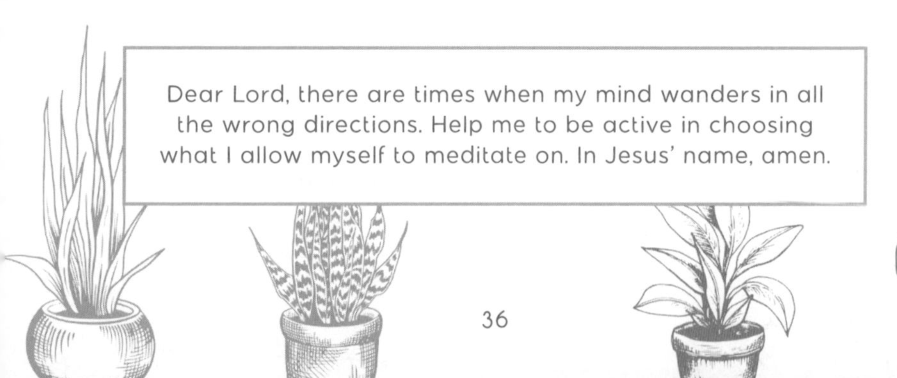

GOING AGAINST THE GRAIN

Jesus said, "If you want to be complete, go, sell what you own, and give the money to the poor. Then you will have treasure in heaven. And come follow me." But when the young man heard this, he went away saddened, because he had many possessions.

MATTHEW 19:21–22 CEB

Oh friend, let's be careful that when we hear God speak to us in the Word and through prayer, we don't become discouraged and choose earthly ways for ease. The truth is that God's path forward is often the hard one because it goes against the grain. It seems counterintuitive, like giving radically to the poor and collecting heavenly treasures. But unless we boldly follow His ways, we won't experience all this life of faith has to offer.

What God asks isn't meant to take away our ability to enjoy life. His commands aren't designed to make us feel in bondage to the boring or enslaved to a dull lifestyle. Instead, righteousness allows for God's blessings. It's a divinely inspired shift in perspective, enabling us to see that His call to surrender all is so we can receive all He has to offer. And, friend, it's always for our good and His glory. Living according to His will is a gift of freedom.

Dear Lord, I'm so glad Your ways and thoughts are higher than mine! Help me to embrace this life of faith, and all it entails, with gusto. In Jesus' name, amen.

WHEN YOU'RE TIRED AND SHAKY

So take a new grip with your tired hands, stand firm on your shaky legs, and mark out a straight, smooth path for your feet so that those who follow you, though weak and lame, will not fall and hurt themselves but become strong.

HEBREWS 12:12–13 TLB

Friend, what has made your hands tired and your legs shaky? What has brought grief or worry into your life? What has depleted you of hope? Where have you been bombarded with spine-weakening challenges? There's no doubt that this world has ways of crowding the joy right out of you. It pushes peace away. And if we're not fighting for balance and making space for God, every day will feel congested with all the wrong things.

Not only can we not afford this emotional clutter for ourselves, but let's remember that others are watching how we navigate this life. If we set an example of self-reliance or hopelessness for our friends and family, they won't see the victorious life that is possible through Jesus. Let's be intentional to fill each day with a strong faith in the only one who can straighten any crooked path and steady our sagging spirit.

Dear Lord, when I begin to feel tired and shaky, let it be a red flag that I'm working in my own strength. My hope is in You—help me to remember this truth every day. In Jesus' name, amen.

CALLED TO BE GENEROUS

"The ax of his judgment is poised over you, ready to sever your roots and cut you down. Yes, every tree that does not produce good fruit will be chopped down and thrown into the fire." The crowd replied, "What do you want us to do?" "If you have two coats," he replied, "give one to the poor. If you have extra food, give it away to those who are hungry."

LUKE 3:9–11 TLB

We're called to be generous. As believers, we're to recognize that what has been given to us is from God. It's His goodness that has blessed us, and our job is to bless others. We're to take care of those who need help. To the world, we are God's hands and feet.

The problem is that we often hoard His gifts for selfish or even judgmental reasons. We aren't financially generous because we want to take care of ourselves. We aren't kind to the downtrodden because we think they've brought it on themselves. We don't give to the beggar on the street corner because we're sure he'll use it the wrong way. But the Word clearly tells us to pour out to others what has been given to us.

If you struggle with giving selflessly, ask the Lord to declutter your heart of worldly ways of thinking and fill it back up with divine generosity.

Dear Lord, help me to be Your hands and feet in thought and deed. In Jesus' name, amen.

WHEN MONEY IS THE PROBLEM

Then Jesus said to his disciples, "I assure you that it will be very hard for a rich person to enter the kingdom of heaven. In fact, it's easier for a camel to squeeze through the eye of a needle than for a rich person to enter God's kingdom." When his disciples heard this, they were stunned. "Then who can be saved?" they asked. Jesus looked at them carefully and said, "It's impossible for human beings. But all things are possible for God."

MATTHEW 19:23–26 CEB

Let's not hear what this passage from the book of Matthew *isn't* saying, friend. Jesus is not declaring that rich people can't go to heaven. Having money doesn't make you a bad person or disqualify you from eternity with God. But we get into trouble when we love our fortunes more than our Father. When we worship the dollar over the divine, the Bible says it's easier to get into heaven by squeezing through the eye of a needle.

Every day, we desperately need to clear away anything that takes the place of God. Instead, we need to fill our hearts with the Word because it's how God reveals Himself to us. Alone, we will never find our eternal home. But through faith, we're assured of eternity.

Dear Lord, let there be nothing in my life that matters more to me than You. In Jesus' name, amen.

THE DETERIORATION OF WHAT MATTERS MOST

The roof sags over the head of lazybones;
the house leaks because of idle hands.
ECCLESIASTES 10:18 VOICE

While this verse from Ecclesiastes is talking about the carelessness of princes in the management of public affairs and how it's destructive to themselves and their people, we can apply this powerful truth to our lives today. By neglecting our responsibilities and being lazy, we'll see a crumbling too. We will see a deterioration of things we hold dear.

This verse challenges us to fill our days wisely. It reminds us of the value and importance of diligent work. God has called us to put our hands to our tasks with purpose and to do so as if we're working for Him. If we sit idle instead, negative results will have free rein to clutter our hearts and homes.

Are there some places where you're seeing this principle play out in your life? Are you investing in things that are meaningless? Are you inactive in relationships that require your input? Do you lack the gumption to get up and go? Maybe it's time to ask God to reignite your awareness of what matters most. Let Him infuse you with new ideas and energy to walk them out. And watch how the Lord opens your eyes and engages your heart in significant ways.

Dear Lord, I confess my carelessness and am excited to embrace the important things again. In Jesus' name, amen.

WHAT FILLS YOUR LIFE?

Try to stay out of all quarrels, and seek to live a clean and holy life, for one who is not holy will not see the Lord. Look after each other so that not one of you will fail to find God's best blessings. Watch out that no bitterness takes root among you, for as it springs up it causes deep trouble, hurting many in their spiritual lives.

HEBREWS 12:14–15 TLB

The world is quick to tell us how to live our best lives. It says to take care of ourselves, look out for number one, do what feels good, find our own truth, and have an open mind. Its advice is jam-packed with ways to be self-focused at all costs. And when we follow that advice, our hearts get cluttered with greediness. It's ugly, and it isn't God's plan for you, friend.

In contrast, today's verses tell us what we are to fill our lives with *instead*. We're to stay out of quarrels, live righteously, point others to God, and live without resentment. This is the opposite of the world's way of living. This is what being others-focused looks like. It's freedom in Christ. It's the choice to be filled to overflowing with love so it spills over into all we do and say.

Dear Lord, please fill me up with love toward others so that they are blessed and You get all the glory! Yes, empower me to live in ways that please You. In Jesus' name, amen.

WHERE IS YOUR TREASURE?

Some people store up treasures in their homes here on earth. This is a shortsighted practice—don't undertake it. Moths and rust will eat up any treasure you may store here. Thieves may break into your homes and steal your precious trinkets. Instead, put up your treasures in heaven where moths do not attack, where rust does not corrode, and where thieves are barred at the door.

MATTHEW 6:19–20 VOICE

Treasure is what we value above all else, and it's what motivates us forward. Wherever we put our focus naturally becomes an influence over the way we act. Maybe we want more money, bigger homes, nicer clothes, fewer wrinkles, newer things, and so on. If we want to hoard earthly treasures, then this is where our time and energy will be spent.

But if we subscribe to the truth in today's verses, wanting to store up our treasures in heaven, then our priorities here and now will be very different. And these treasures will be "evergreen"—they will last forever rather than corrode and crumble.

Friend, our hearts are in a tug-of-war. The world's offerings are nice and shiny. And while many of us say heaven is our focus, the reality is that our hearts often say something else. Where is your treasure?

Dear Lord, I want to store up my treasures in heaven. Please help me to walk that out today. In Jesus' name, amen.

THE VALUE OF PEACE

A dry crust eaten in peace is better than steak every day along with argument and strife.
PROVERBS 17:1 TLB

Let's be honest. Taking a big bite of dry crust holds no appeal to anyone. Not only is it tough, but it's probably also flavorless. Today's verse reveals that having peace is such a wonderful gift, it can make even that unappetizing bite of stale bread taste good. Living in harmony is beyond all other blessings.

In contrast, many of us would love to feast on a juicy steak. Maybe your mouth is watering right now, thinking of a perfectly seasoned grilled filet mignon. But the writer of this proverb tells us that such a morsel is unappealing when it's accompanied by arguments and strife.

It's important that we fill our homes and hearts with peace. It's so valuable, in fact, that it will make up for the loss of other comforts. Better to have calm and serenity in the lacking than to be cluttered by strife in the luxuries.

What is the Holy Spirit speaking to you right now? Are there places where you need to make some changes so peace is a priority? Have you been suffocated by fighting and discord? Ask God to show you where to clean out the conflict and replace it with calm.

Dear Lord, would You open my eyes to what needs to change and show me how to pursue peace in my life? In Jesus' name, amen.

A SPECIAL NEARNESS

Go down to the people and get them ready to meet Me today and tomorrow by purifying themselves and washing their garments. By the third day, they need to be ready, for on that day I will descend from Mount Sinai so that everyone can see.

EXODUS 19:10–11 VOICE

While on the mountain in God's presence, Moses was commanded to get the people of Israel cleaned up and ready because the Lord was coming down to meet with them. Yes, God had been a travel companion during their wilderness time, but the Israelites were about to experience a special nearness to the Lord.

They were instructed to purify themselves and clean their clothes. It was spiritual preparation and bodily purification. Chances are many of us were told to wash behind our ears and put on our Sunday best for church, so maybe, in a way, we can understand the importance of this command. The Israelites were purging impurities so they could stand before a holy God.

Friend, what sins are crowding you today? What impurities are squeezing out your faith? As you pray, take time to confess and repent, removing anything that might keep you from experiencing a special nearness to the Lord.

Dear Lord, help me to purge any impurities that might keep me from a deeper relationship with You. I long to spend time with You through prayer and time in the Word. In Jesus' name, amen.

INCREASE, NOT DECREASE

This is what the Lord of Armies, the God of Israel, says to all those who were taken captive from Jerusalem to Babylon: Build houses, and live in them. Plant gardens, and eat what they produce. Get married, and have sons and daughters. Find wives for your sons, and let your daughters get married so that they can have sons and daughters. Grow in number there; don't decrease. Work for the good of the city where I've taken you as captives, and pray to the Lord for that city. When it prospers, you will also prosper.

Jeremiah 29:4–7 GW

Jeremiah was making sure the Israelites knew their time in Babylon would be substantial. This wasn't going to be a long weekend away from home. No one would be rushing in to save them. And if they were interested in their own comfort and prosperity, they needed to inhabit their place of captivity in ways that were beneficial for the long term. In other words, they were to increase and not decrease.

We can do the same here. While earth isn't our final home, we can live here with passion and purpose, filling each day with faith and meaning as we wait for eternity. We can increase in the Lord's goodness and shine His light into the darkness.

Dear Lord, help me to live my life here with purpose and passion. In Jesus' name, amen.

FILLING YOUR HEART WITH TRUTH

Therefore, let us all be thankful that we are a part of an unshakable Kingdom and offer to God worship that pleases Him and reflects the awe and reverence we have toward Him, for He is like a fierce fire that consumes everything.

HEBREWS 12:28–29 VOICE

When we think about our amazing Father in heaven, we are called to have a grateful heart and to offer pleasing worship that reflects our respect and reverence. But sometimes when He comes to mind, our thoughts are cluttered with shame for our sins, anger because we don't understand His ways, and doubt that He is who He says He is and will do what He says He'll do. Rather than embrace God's goodness, we refute it.

But the reality is that faith is active. Faith chooses to believe He is unchangeable, and His kingdom, unshakable. It chooses to trust Him enough to be thankful even when we don't yet see the answered prayer. It chooses to look forward with everlasting hope when things feel impossible. Faith remembers that God is good all the time, regardless of what life brings our way. And it acknowledges that the Lord is sovereign and His will most certainly will be done. Fill your heart with these truths.

Dear Lord, my heart is full of gratitude as I meditate on Your goodness toward me in every way. Help me to choose by faith to please You every day. In Jesus' name, amen.

CROWD YOURSELF WITH CHRIST

"Only be strong and very courageous, faithfully doing everything in the teachings that my servant Moses commanded you. Don't turn away from them. Then you will succeed wherever you go. Never stop reciting these teachings. You must think about them night and day so that you will faithfully do everything written in them. Only then will you prosper and succeed."

JOSHUA 1:7–8 GW

If your mind is going to be cluttered with anything, clutter it with God's Word. Pack your heart full of scripture that saturates those deep places inside where your spirit feels restless. Stuff yourself with the goodness of the Lord's promises so worry and fear stay at bay. Cram as many of His truths into your head as you can manage so they become the lens through which you view life.

The problem is that we have allowed the world to litter our hearts with lies and limitations, leading us into hopelessness. We've willingly walked down paths that have effectively destroyed our peace and robbed us of joy. Starting today, let's instead choose to crowd ourselves with Christ and meditate on His goodness. By doing so, we will find prosperity and success in meaningful ways.

Dear Lord, I confess the times I've filled up on what the world has to offer rather than feasting on Your promises. Change my focus and my heart. In Jesus' name, amen.

GOD KNOWS

I know the plans that I have for you, declares the L*ORD*.
They are plans for peace and not disaster, plans to give you a future filled with hope.

JEREMIAH 29:11 GW

Too often, we get weighed down by our circumstances and go into fix-it mode. We carry the burden on our shoulders as we try to navigate the ups and downs of life, forgetting that God already knows our future. He knows what's ahead because He's planned it. The Lord also knows how everything will turn out. Yet we get caught up in trying to manage it all on our own, without asking for help from the only one who can encourage and guide us through.

Friend, how does it make you feel to read today's verse and know that the Lord has spent time creating plans for your life? Even more, these plans are for peace and not chaos. They are for harmony and not adversity. And they are for a future filled with hope. If you will seek Him in those hard times and purge the desire to work in your own strength, then you will find the energy and wisdom you need.

Dear Lord, what a blessing to know You have put my future together with love and purpose. You know everything that's headed my way and how it will turn out in the end. And I can trust You to walk through it with me. Thank You for loving me so completely! In Jesus' name, amen.

SEEKING GOD FIRST

But you, who are devoted to being with God and searching for God, be strong and do not lose courage because your actions will reap rewards.

2 CHRONICLES 15:7 VOICE

When we press into God rather than freak out about difficult circumstances, we are flexing our faith. Every time we bow our head in prayer when hit with hard news, rather than call our best friend, we reveal faith in the Father. And when we feel hopeless and unsure of how to move forward in trials and search the scriptures for direction, we show we trust in God above ourselves. This is good. This is courage. This is devotion.

As believers, we must be careful to fill up in the right places. The world's advice isn't sound. Societal trends aren't steady or lasting. Unsaved friends and family can't offer the godly advice we need. And those who do have saving faith process life through their humanity. Even with the best intentions, their advice can clutter our hearts in unhelpful ways. Friend, we need God alone to speak into those parched places. And when we seek Him first, according to scripture, blessings will follow.

Dear Lord, I have faith in You, but I admit there are times I look to the world for insight and ideas for how to process life. Sometimes I look everywhere but in Your Word. I talk it out with everyone but You. Forgive me. Help my heart to seek only Your wisdom. In Jesus' name, amen.

GOD'S CLEAR COMMANDS

"Haven't I commanded you? Strength! Courage! Don't be timid; don't get discouraged. God, your God, is with you every step you take."
JOSHUA 1:9 MSG

This verse from the book of Joshua is a powerful directive, friend. But maybe there are times we read God's Word and decide His commands are merely suggestions. Without realizing it, we soften the Lord's mandates in our minds. We diminish His decrees or refuse to accept the gravity of His directives. Sometimes we don't take a command seriously because we don't think it applies to us here and now. But when God powerfully and clearly commands something of believers, we need to respond in obedience. If we don't, we are choosing to turn our backs on Him in defiance.

Throughout the Bible, the Lord instructs those who love Him to exhibit strength and courage. . .not fear and worry. This instruction is also for us today. And we can't obey it by just trying harder or working smarter. Instead, God knows we can only walk out this command with His help. And as we are intentional to remove excuses and misunderstandings and to fill our hearts with faith and trust in Him, strength and courage will be a natural outflow.

Dear Lord, I confess that I've willfully overlooked some of Your clear commands in the Bible. I've chosen not to see them as applying to me, or I've made excuses as to why I can't obey. Help me instead to understand that Your commands are always for me and that blessings will flow from obedience. In Jesus' name, amen.

WHO IS MOLDING YOU?

Do not allow this world to mold you in its own image. Instead, be transformed from the inside out by renewing your mind. As a result, you will be able to discern what God wills and whatever God finds good, pleasing, and complete.

ROMANS 12:2 VOICE

When you spend time in God's Word, you will become transformed from the inside out. Sitting with scripture and meditating on it will cause it to supernaturally penetrate your heart and bring about powerful change. Soaking in the Word daily will renew your mind and clear away the debris left by subscribing to the world's ways, which have been insignificant at best and destructive at worst.

Little by little, day by day, your faith will mature. It will grow with the help of God's Holy Spirit living in you. He will open your eyes to truth and help you begin to discern what is good and pleasing—and what is not.

So, friend, think about it. Who is molding you today? Is your heart being squeezed in worldly ways, or are you seeking the Lord's guidance in all things? Are you falling prey to culture or being renewed by Christ? It's your choice every day.

Dear Lord, the world's voice is loud, and its influence, powerful. Many times I've let it clutter my heart with all the wrong things. Help me to seek You through the Word and in prayer so I'm able to see Your truth and stand on it. In Jesus' name, amen.

BEING A GOOD AND GODLY LEADER

They should manage their own household well—
they should see that their children are obedient with complete respect, because if they don't know how to manage their own household, how can they take care of God's church?

1 Timothy 3:4–5 CEB

This scripture describes, in part, the qualities needed for someone to be considered an overseer of the church. These people should have deep honor and reverence for God and be upstanding members of the community. For the appointment of these leaders, the mandate was to find those whose lives were filled with integrity rather than littered with fleshly desires. Their priorities needed to be in the right order. Their hearts needed to be turned toward the Lord.

Being a good and godly leader takes intentionality. No matter what kind of leadership role we may fill, when life gets messy, we're called to remain steady and faithful. Whether we're leading our family, a company, a volunteer effort, or a small group, we must be careful to keep our hearts clear of worldly ways. Our hearts—our thoughts—should be seeking God's will each step of the way. And we can walk this out by anchoring ourselves to His Word and listening for His wisdom and guidance. It's not always easy, but it's always worth it.

Dear Lord, help me to thrive as I lead because I'm deeply rooted in Your truth. Help me to seek You in each decision. Help me to be resolved, yet loving, as I guide and direct. In Jesus' name, amen.

SEEKING GOD ABOVE ALL ELSE

In those days when you pray, I will listen. You will find me when you seek me, if you look for me in earnest. Yes, says the Lord, I will be found by you, and I will end your slavery and restore your fortunes; I will gather you out of the nations where I sent you and bring you back home again to your own land.

JEREMIAH 29:12–14 TLB

Sometimes we have so much clutter in our lives that we can't clearly see our need for God. We become overly busy with work and home commitments—and without our realizing it, He falls off our radar. When we hit difficult patches, rather than seek the Lord, we seek the advice of our parents, our husbands, our friends. . .or numb ourselves to escape the situation we're struggling with. Our faith is crowded out by our fear and the drive to figure things out on our own. And eventually, we get to the end of ourselves and look up.

Friend, let today's verses wash over you with a sweet reminder that God is waiting for you to cry out. He's listening. And when you call on Him, He promises to be found. The Lord will hear you and act. He will surround you with His presence and meet your needs in meaningful ways.

Dear Lord, hear my voice crying out to You right now. Meet me in this parched place. In Jesus' name, amen.

NO IDOLS

You are not to serve any other gods before Me. You are not to make any idol or image of other gods. In fact, you are not to make an image of anything in the heavens above, on the earth below, or in the waters beneath. You are not to bow down and serve any image, for I, the Eternal your God, am a jealous God. As for those who are not loyal to Me, their children will endure the consequences of their sins for three or four generations.

EXODUS 20:3–5 VOICE

Today's passage is part of the Ten Commandments, the rules that God gave to Moses to share with the Israelites. He had just rescued the nation from slavery, bringing them into the wilderness and calling them His treasured possession. He also told them to purge any worldly impurities and devote themselves only to Him. But they didn't do a good job of following His instruction.

The truth is that our God is a jealous God, and He commands us to fill our hearts so full of Him that there's no room for any kind of idol to squeeze out our faith. And that includes anything, anywhere—be it heavenly or earthly. When you begin to elevate something or someone above God, let it be a red flag.

Dear Lord, I confess there are idols I've allowed to take first place in my heart. Help me to better understand when I'm doing this so I can stay focused only on You. In Jesus' name, amen.

CLUTTERED BY PRIDE?

Because of the kindness that God has shown me, I ask you not to think of yourselves more highly than you should. Instead, your thoughts should lead you to use good judgment based on what God has given each of you as believers.

ROMANS 12:3 GW

When today's verse says "based on what God has given," it's a reminder that we can't collect and store up pride because our individual measures of faith come from Him. He alone determines the measure of our faith, not our efforts or actions. Faith is the first gift we receive after being born again, and it's what brings our other giftings to life through the work of the Holy Spirit.

Unfortunately, pride is part of the human condition, and it pushes out the truth of how good God is to us. It makes us the hero. It gives us all the credit. And it says we're worthy of praise and recognition for the state of our faith. Let's not forget that scripture clearly states it also comes right before our fall.

As believers, we can't be in both camps. Either faith comes from God, or we work for it and it's dependent on what we do. Make sure your heart is filled with the truth that faith is a gift given to us as He determines. Our response is gratitude and stewardship.

Dear Lord, thank You for the gift of faith and for the Holy Spirit's commitment to mature it with care. In Jesus' name, amen.

INVADED BY SELF-FOCUSED THOUGHTS

But Martha was the jittery type and was worrying over the big dinner she was preparing. She came to Jesus and said, "Sir, doesn't it seem unfair to you that my sister just sits here while I do all the work? Tell her to come and help me." But the Lord said to her, "Martha, dear friend, you are so upset over all these details! There is really only one thing worth being concerned about. Mary has discovered it—and I won't take it away from her!"

LUKE 10:40–42 TLB

Imagine the thoughts bombarding Martha as she stewed in the kitchen that day. She was busy at work while Mary sat. Maybe you've experienced something similar and can understand all the emotions swirling around. But notice what Martha eventually did. She took her frustrations to the Lord.

What a powerful reminder that while we will feel invaded by self-focused thoughts from time to time, we have freedom to take them straight to the Lord. He will help us sort them out. He will remove them. And He will lovingly reorder our hearts and reaffirm the depth of His love for us, even when we're messy.

Dear Lord, I can relate to Martha and her irritation over this situation. I can even see those times happening in my life too. Thank You for reminding me that You care about my hurts and hang-ups. In Jesus' name, amen.

SACRIFICIAL LOVE

Love sincerely. Hate evil. Hold on to what is good. Be devoted to each other like a loving family. Excel in showing respect for each other. Don't be lazy in showing your devotion. Use your energy to serve the Lord. Be happy in your confidence, be patient in trouble, and pray continually. Share what you have with God's people who are in need. Be hospitable.

ROMANS 12:9–13 GW

In this section of Romans, Paul is unpacking what sacrificial love in community looks like. He tells them—is telling us—to hold on to what is good because that's how we keep evil from infiltrating the heart. Evil is the enemy of all that God stands for. Paul is rightly telling believers to fill themselves with moral decency and to love others well, something we can only do through faith. As we cling to God for help to walk out these commands, He transforms us through the process and enables us to live righteously.

Yes, this process is hard! We're surrounded by a sinful and selfish world every day, and that's why we need the Lord's help. But when loving others well is our hearts' desire and we seek His leading, we will be a blessing to those around us.

Dear Lord, there's no doubt I need Your help to walk out sacrificial love in community. I cannot do this without You. Please help me to hold on to all that is good, especially when it's challenging. In Jesus' name, amen.

PACK YOUR LIFE WITH LOVE

You should love Him, your True God, with all your heart and soul, with every ounce of your strength. Make the things I'm commanding you today part of who you are. Repeat them to your children. Talk about them when you're sitting together in your home and when you're walking together down the road. Make them the last thing you talk about before you go to bed and the first thing you talk about the next morning. Do whatever it takes to remember them: tie a reminder on your hand and bind a reminder on your forehead where you'll see it all the time.

DEUTERONOMY 6:5–8 VOICE

Moses didn't mince words. He was very clear as he instructed the Israelites to remember God's commands once they crossed the Jordan River and took the land He had promised them. Simply put, they were to fill their hearts and souls to overflowing with love for God. Whatever else had been crowding their commitment, this was the time to flush out the wrong things and refill with the right things. In every way, the Lord wanted to see the depth of their adoration and appreciation.

Friend, this command is also for today's believers. We're instructed to live in ways that bring God glory. In our words and actions, He wants us to pack our lives with love so we will see the blessing in generations to come.

Dear Lord, I love You! In Jesus' name, amen.

TOO BUSY LOVING YOURSELF?

Bless those who persecute you. Bless them, and don't curse them. Be happy with those who are happy. Be sad with those who are sad. Live in harmony with each other. Don't be arrogant, but be friendly to humble people. Don't think that you are smarter than you really are.

ROMANS 12:14–16 GW

Sometimes we clutter our lives with all the wrong things, like pride. Oh friend, this is something we all struggle with. It's an equal-opportunity sin that crowds out our love for others because we're too busy loving ourselves. We're busy picking up offenses and stirring up chaos. And rather than be a blessing to those around us and a peacemaker in our community, we are reckless in relationships.

It's hard to show compassion when we're full of criticism. We can't love when we're preoccupied with loathing. We can't promote harmony when we're filled with hate. How can we be friendly when we're gripped with fear that others may be better than we are? Friend, let's choose to be women who store up kindness and share it. Let's be so full of God's goodness that it overflows into the lives of those we love. If we're too busy with anything, let it be blessing our community and living our faith boldly.

Dear Lord, fill my heart with the desire to love and bless others with purpose and passion. In Jesus' name, amen.

SAYING NO TO THE THINGS WE WANT

Then Jesus called the crowd to himself along with his disciples. He said to them, "Those who want to follow me must say no to the things they want, pick up their crosses, and follow me. Those who want to save their lives will lose them. But those who lose their lives for me and for the Good News will save them."

MARK 8:34–35 GW

Today's scripture reminds us that to follow the Lord, we must off-load what keeps us self-centered. Focusing on fulfilling our own desires can't be what drives us each day if we want to live a faithful and righteous life. We must be willing to give up greediness to gain godliness. We are called to empty ourselves of anything that takes our eyes off Jesus. And when we do, we will be saved through faith. But even then, choosing to follow God's will over our own is a daily decision for every believer.

Where do your priorities need to be adjusted? What is the Holy Spirit showing you that needs to change? Where are you too self-seeking rather than Jesus-seeking? Where do you need to say no to the things you want more than God?

Dear Lord, help me to clearly see that You are more important than anything the world can offer to satisfy. May I say no to my wants so I can say yes to You. In Jesus' name, amen.

SEEING THE BIGGER PICTURE

Teach us to number our days and recognize how few they are; help us to spend them as we should.
PSALM 90:12 TLB

Maybe you're in a season right now that's littered with challenges and heartaches. And it doesn't feel like the days are few; instead, they seem to linger longer than feels good. There's no doubt we can all relate to those parched places.

Is your marriage crumbling under the weight of unforgiveness? Did your child fall prey to the many lies the world has been whispering in his ear—the ones you didn't even know about? Do the bills continue to pile up, day after day, with no end in sight? Are you waiting for God to heal you or someone you love? Do you feel unseen and hopeless in your plight of trying to get pregnant or find a husband? Have the past few years of struggles left you paralyzed and unable to move forward in confidence?

God is inviting you to focus your eyes on Him rather than allowing your heart to be cluttered by these earthly trials. It won't make them disappear, but your heart will see the bigger picture of eternity in ways that will settle your spirit in the here and now.

Dear Lord, help me to take my eyes off my struggles and train them on You for perspective and hope. I need Your guidance now more than ever. In Jesus' name, amen.

THE HOLY SPIRIT

"If you love me, obey me; and I will ask the Father and he will give you another Comforter, and he will never leave you. He is the Holy Spirit, the Spirit who leads into all truth. The world at large cannot receive him, for it isn't looking for him and doesn't recognize him. But you do, for he lives with you now and some day shall be in you."

JOHN 14:15–17 TLB

For believers, the Holy Spirit is our comforter, counselor, advocate, and helper. He's a gift we receive when we're born again, and his continual presence is one of the most important characteristics that defines a Christian. The world cannot understand the value the Spirit brings into our lives.

The Spirit makes us holy and activates our ability to walk out a life of faith. He lives in us, making us God's temple and helping to push out the worldly ways we've embraced. And we're assured that He will never leave us but will continue to abide in us until we see Jesus face-to-face.

When we begin to feel the old ways creep in and crowd us once again, He will set off alarm bells so we can realign our hearts with His. The Spirit will bring a sweet conviction and guidance to keep our faith steady.

Dear Lord, thank You for the gift of the Holy Spirit and His work in my life. In Jesus' name, amen.

PURGING THE DESIRE FOR REVENGE

Don't pay people back with evil for the evil they do to you.
Focus your thoughts on those things that are considered noble.
As much as it is possible, live in peace with everyone.

ROMANS 12:17–18 GW

Did you notice in this passage the words "as much as it is possible"? This means it's not always possible to live in peace with others, and it's a good reminder that sometimes our best efforts will fall flat. Our heart may have been in the right place, but theirs wasn't. Anytime we run into that situation, confident we did our best with pure motives, we can't let our heart be littered with lies saying we failed.

It's not easy to silence the voice that tells us to repay evil with evil. We want others to feel the pain they inflicted on us. We want them to understand they messed up. And we want to know that they got what was coming to them. Friend, we are wretched without Jesus.

But His command is to focus our mind on things that are noble and good. Things that are true and right, beautiful and honorable. Because when we do, the desire for revenge will be purged. There just won't be room in our heart for it. And as a result, we'll have a divine perspective characterized by His goodness, love, and faithfulness.

Dear Lord, please give me a heart for peace. In Jesus' name, amen.

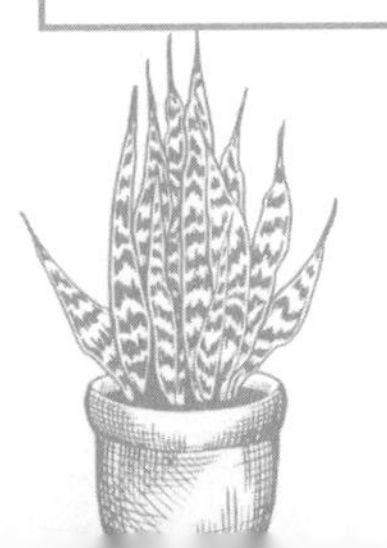

HOW YOU CAN SHOW LOVE TO GOD

Anyone who loves Me will listen to My voice and obey. The Father will love him, and We will draw close to him and make a dwelling place within him. The one who does not love Me ignores My message, which is not from Me, but from the Father who sent Me.

JOHN 14:23–24 VOICE

Let's be intentional to remove anything that prevents us from living in obedience to God's will. This is one way we show our love for Him. And it opens up a storehouse of blessings, including the mighty gift of His presence.

Ask the Holy Spirit to show you places of disobedience, and He will. Are you hoarding unforgiveness in your marriage? Is there unchecked anger toward a rebellious teen? Are you living in sinful ways you know aren't pleasing to the Lord? Have you shown a lack of wisdom and self-control in your finances? Are you filled with jealousy or actively betraying someone who trusts you? Has worry or anxiety cluttered your heart? Or are you allowing fear to keep you from walking out the calling God has placed on your life?

Friend, listen for His voice speaking to you right now. . .and obey. If you're unsure if it's His voice, let the Bible confirm it, because they will not contradict each other. Your choice to follow reveals your faith while also showing God your love.

Dear Lord, I will listen and obey. In Jesus' name, amen.

GOD APPRECIATES ORDER

Complete your work outside, and get your fields ready for next season; after that's done, build your house.

PROVERBS 24:27 VOICE

Knowing that God appreciates order is so comforting. After all, as women, we often find that order is essential to getting through our day. From car pool to meal prep to work deadlines to home management, being organized is how we make it all happen. It keeps our minds focused and our progress on track so we can avoid unnecessary stress. And with so many people depending on us for a sense of calm and stability, we can feel safe going to the Lord for help because we know He understands.

Do you need God to help declutter the mayhem in your life today? Do you struggle to tame the turmoil when you wake up each morning? Does your to-do list feel overwhelming, bringing on anxiety as you try to work through it? God sees you.

Spend time today telling Him about your frustrations and the places where you can't find peace. Open up about where you feel like a failure, certain you're letting people down along the way. And then ask the Lord to help you order your steps in ways that settle your spirit and fill you with hope rather than keeping you tangled in disarray.

Dear Lord, my best efforts at order are falling flat. I can't find my way through each day with a peaceful heart. Please show me how to arrange my responsibilities so I can be most effective. In Jesus' name, amen.

IT'S ABOUT THE HEART

He has told you, mortals, what is good in His sight.
What else does the Eternal ask of you but to live justly and to love kindness and to walk with your True God in all humility?
MICAH 6:8 VOICE

This chapter in Micah is an imaginary conversation between God and the nation of Israel. The first five verses are His examples of their disobedience followed by a series of questions they are asking in response. Today's verse is the Lord's reply, essentially exposing Israel's need for a change of heart. The people's lives were cluttered by the law, but God wanted their heartfelt compliance. He didn't desire their religiosity but rather their adoration and love.

Today, He wants the same from us. We're to go beyond merely following rules and embrace the life God wants for us. To live justly means to have a proper sense of right and wrong. To love kindness means to be genuine and generous to others and loyal to the Lord. And to walk in humility means to have a right attitude toward God, depending on Him above our own abilities.

Ask Him to reveal where you may be rule following rather than wholeheartedly doing what you know is good and pleasing in the Lord's sight—because there is a difference.

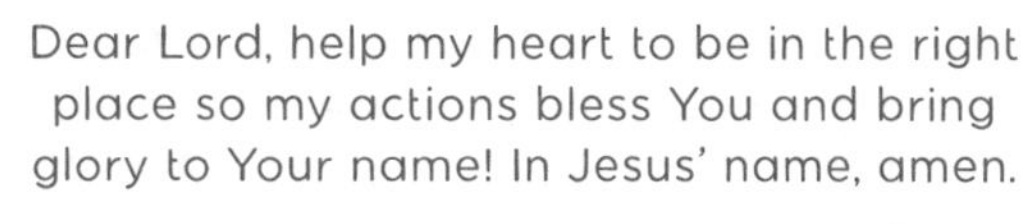

VERTICAL AND HORIZONTAL

Whoever pursues justice and treats others with kindness
discovers true life marked by integrity and respect.

PROVERBS 21:21 VOICE

The kind of life referenced here in Proverbs 21 is lived with great intention and is solidly anchored to righteousness. It requires a daily pursuit of God's help and a heart surrendered to His will. It also requires a deep love and respect in relationships with others so that kindness comes through unhindered. These two types of connections are known as "vertical" and "horizontal," respectively.

The problem for many of us is that we're so full of our own efforts that we don't make room for God's strength and guidance. We rely on ourselves more. Our default is to try to handle things on our own. And that mindset ensures that we underutilize the vertical relationship that empowers the horizontal one, leaving us ineffective all the way around.

Today, commit to reestablishing your bond with the Lord. Make reading the Bible a daily habit, knowing that God speaks through His Word to every believer who seeks Him. Be prayerful, thanking Him for the goodness shown to you and for the strength to live a life marked by integrity and respect.

Dear Lord, I know You are the key to a life well lived and one that glorifies Your holy name. Help me to pursue You every day so I'm empowered to be who You created me to be. In Jesus' name, amen.

FILLING YOUR MIND WITH HEAVEN

Let heaven fill your thoughts; don't spend your time worrying about things down here. You should have as little desire for this world as a dead person does. Your real life is in heaven with Christ and God. And when Christ who is our real life comes back again, you will shine with him and share in all his glories.

COLOSSIANS 3:2–4 TLB

Paul tells us to fill our thoughts with heavenly things because nothing the world has to offer is worthy of that space. The here and now isn't our final destination. Earthly treasures pale in comparison to eternal ones. And even more, our desire for the world should be nonexistent. How could Paul be any clearer?

Yet many of us still hold on to worrying about our marriages and our children, or lack thereof. We feel anxious about the condition of our finances and our health. Fear surrounds the thought of losing those we love or stuff we have accumulated. We're stressed about climbing the ladder of success or never getting what we really want in this lifetime. And probably a million other things too. But when we focus on these things, we're forgetting the truth that our real life is in heaven—not here.

As a believer, you are destined to shine with the Lord in glory!

Dear Lord, thank You for the reminder that my real life is with You in heaven. In Jesus' name, amen.

DECLUTTERING THE DARKNESS

"You are the world's light—a city on a hill, glowing in the night for all to see. Don't hide your light! Let it shine for all; let your good deeds glow for all to see, so that they will praise your heavenly Father."
MATTHEW 5:14–16 TLB

The light of Jesus that shines from every believer helps to declutter the world of darkness. It pushes it aside and fills the void with God's goodness. The way we live and the words we speak create a godly glow for all to see. When done right, those things point to the Father in heaven, giving Him glory and praise.

But when we hide our faith or fail to speak up, our light dims. When we promote chaos and hold on to unforgiveness, the radiance diminishes. When we're embarrassed about being a believer or live in unrepentant sin, the dark can squeeze out the light. When we're racked with worry and choked by fear, the brightness fades. Friend, this isn't God's plan for our lives. Don't choose it.

Instead, let's be bold for Jesus! This world's darkness is only going to get darker, but our confidence in shining for the Lord will help bring more hearts to His goodness and a saving faith. Together, we can make a dent in the dark and help crowd it out.

> Dear Lord, help me to be a bright light through the way I live my life each day. In Jesus' name, amen.

FIRST AND FOREMOST

So, first and foremost, I urge God's people to pray.
They should make their requests, petitions, and thanksgivings
on behalf of all humanity. Teach them to pray for kings
(or anyone in high places for that matter) so that we can
lead quiet, peaceful lives—reverent, godly, and holy.
1 TIMOTHY 2:1–2 VOICE

How might your day be different if you filled it with prayers first and foremost? Rather than expecting the world to provide insight and strength for battle, what if you took those petitions straight to God? Starting your day with prayers of thanksgiving helps to set your mind on eternal things rather than earthly ones. And when you pack those prayers with everything that's on your heart—from the challenges facing your friends and family, to the happenings in your community and state, to the leaders in our nation and world—fear is kept at bay. Worry can't easily take root, and you will navigate your day in peace.

Let's be women of prayer not only because we're told to be but because we understand the blessings that come from it. Let's be intentional to satiate our hearts with the presence of God as we get moving each morning. And then let's carry that posture with us until we close our eyes at night.

Dear Lord, let me be a woman who prays with purpose and passion. In Jesus' name, amen.

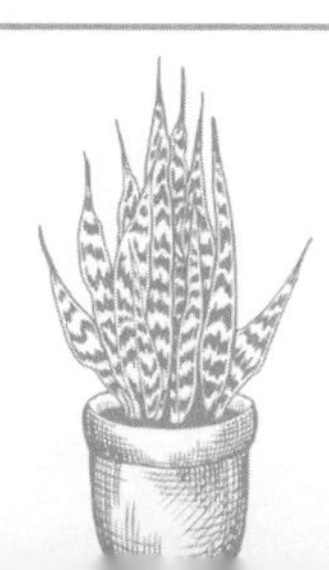

WHEN LOVING AND PRAYING FOR ENEMIES IS HARD

"There is a saying, 'Love your friends and hate your enemies.' But I say: Love your enemies! Pray for those who persecute you! . . . If you love only those who love you, what good is that? Even scoundrels do that much. If you are friendly only to your friends, how are you different from anyone else? Even the heathen do that."

MATTHEW 5:43–44, 46–47 TLB

Friend, the truth is we can only love our enemies when our hearts are full of God! Left to our strength, we can't possibly love our adversaries genuinely. . .at least not for long. We won't be able to pray for them with pure motives either. And if we were honest, we'd have to admit that sometimes our minds are cluttered with terrible thoughts and feelings toward those we consider enemies. Jesus' command is counterintuitive and feels impossible on every level. That's why we need to ask the Lord for help. We simply cannot love others well without Him.

Today, think of someone who you need God's help to love and forgive. Who is the Holy Spirit nudging you to pray for? Talk to Him about it. Be the kind of woman whose life is guided by Jesus' example of selfless surrender and steadfast faith. Be the blessing you were born to be, even when others don't deserve it.

Dear Lord, help me to love and pray for my enemies, especially when it's hard. In Jesus' name, amen.

IT'S TIME TO LIVE DIFFERENTLY

Away then with sinful, earthly things; deaden the evil desires lurking within you; have nothing to do with sexual sin, impurity, lust, and shameful desires; don't worship the good things of life, for that is idolatry. God's terrible anger is upon those who do such things. You used to do them when your life was still part of this world; but now is the time to cast off and throw away all these rotten garments of anger, hatred, cursing, and dirty language.

Colossians 3:5–8 TLB

Today's verses remind us of something very important. Before we accepted Jesus into our hearts and became His faithful followers, we didn't understand the weight of our sin. We didn't have the Holy Spirit to reveal the evil and shameful desires stirring inside us. Without a second thought, we made idols of earthly things and often obsessed over trying to stay relevant. And we tried to meet every fleshly craving because we didn't know any better. But now is the time to live differently.

As believers, we can no longer be cluttered by worldly ways or wants. That's old behavior, unbecoming of us now that we've said yes to the Lord. Our lives should point others to God in heaven instead.

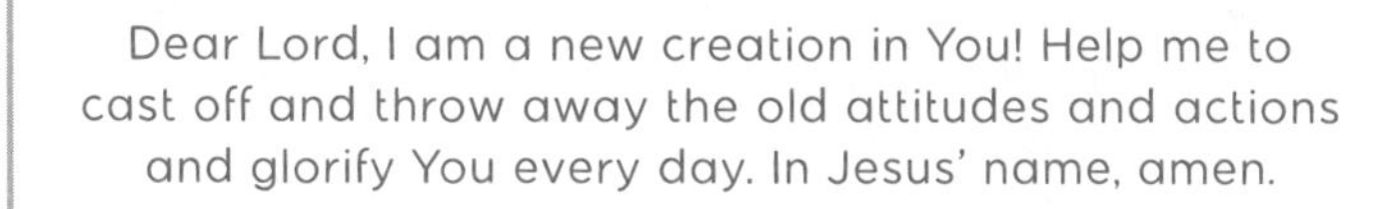

CHASING WITH PASSION

Timothy, run away from youthful desires. Instead, direct your passion to chasing after righteousness, faithfulness, love, and peace, along with those who call upon the Lord with pure hearts.

2 TIMOTHY 2:22 VOICE

What if we were to direct our passion toward chasing after the things listed in this verse? What if living for the Lord received our greatest effort? What if loving others, being peacemakers, living faithfully, and seeking a right relationship with God were daily pursuits? The world would be a much better place, that's for sure!

The reality is that it's difficult at best to walk out these instructions—especially when we try on our own. We may be very capable women in many ways, but we're significantly limited by our humanity. Living this way takes the Lord's daily strength, wisdom, and grace. . .and our surrender to following His will and ways above our own.

Today, why not recommit your life to God and be filled to the brim with His goodness? Find encouragement in today's verse, letting it infuse you and give you renewed purpose as a believer. When you choose to fully embrace what it means to chase after your faith with passion, watch how God will bring blessings to you—and to others through you.

Dear Lord, help me to direct my passion to chasing after things with an eternal value. My faith in You matters to me, and I need Your help to live it out well each day. In Jesus' name, amen.

BEING SPIRITUALLY FIT

Bodily exercise is all right, but spiritual exercise is much more important and is a tonic for all you do. So exercise yourself spiritually, and practice being a better Christian because that will help you not only now in this life, but in the next life too.

1 TIMOTHY 4:8 TLB

Based on today's verse, how do you practice being a better Christian? How do you exercise yourself spiritually? This is a purposeful investment in your relationship with God, designed to strengthen your faith muscle for the battles that lie ahead—the ones this sinful and selfish world will bring your way. So how do you do it?

One of the best ways we get trained for battle is by spending concentrated time in God's Word every day. It prepares us from the inside out, helping us discern right from wrong and truth from lies. Another way is by going to the Lord in prayer right when the struggle begins, because His presence brings peace and perspective. And we can also surround ourselves with godly community, ensuring that our faith stays in shape.

Friend, every bit of time spent in His presence helps keep evil from littering our thoughts so righteousness can't be pushed out.

Dear Lord, I want my heart and mind to be exercised spiritually so that I'm fully saturated in Your Word and Your presence, making me fit and ready for whatever life throws my way. In Jesus' name, amen.

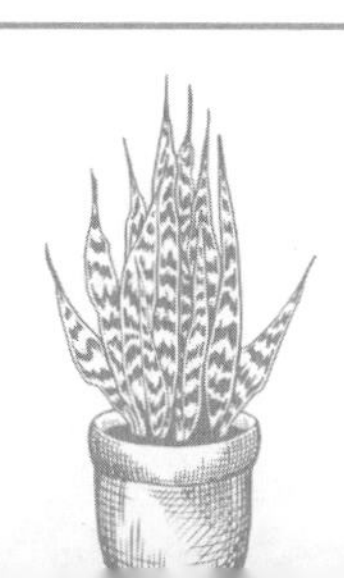

YOUR FAITH PLEASES GOD

You can never please God without faith, without depending on him. Anyone who wants to come to God must believe that there is a God and that he rewards those who sincerely look for him.

HEBREWS 11:6 TLB

Your faith in the Father matters. The world may call it nonsense. . .or suggest there are many gods to believe in. . .or say all roads lead to Him, so do what makes you happy. But the truth is that there's only one true God, and we find our way to Him through His Son, Jesus. His death on the cross paid for our sins once and for all, and then He rose three days later. Choosing to follow Jesus—being born again—secures the Holy Spirit's presence within us and our eternity in heaven.

Never underestimate the power of belief. Without it, our faith is powerless. When we surrender to the Lord, acknowledging His sovereignty and our sinfulness, He is pleased! And it's through our relationship with Him that we're able to live in ways that bring Him glory. As we seek the Lord each day, we'll experience the blessings of His goodness. The earthly clutter in our lives will be replaced by the eternal consecrations of God.

Dear Lord, I believe in You. I believe in the salvation work Jesus did for me on the cross. And as a believer, I am thankful for the Holy Spirit who lives in me. In Jesus' name, amen.

NEW CLOTHES

Don't lie to one another. You're done with that old life. It's like a filthy set of ill-fitting clothes you've stripped off and put in the fire. Now you're dressed in a new wardrobe. Every item of your new way of life is custom-made by the Creator, with his label on it. All the old fashions are now obsolete.

COLOSSIANS 3:9–10 MSG

Let your new, custom-made wardrobe crowd out the old, filthy one because those clothes don't fit anymore. In other words, you are a new creation in Christ, and the old ways of living are gone. Your faith in Jesus is transformative, so embrace it with gusto!

As a believer, look at your life and recognize the beautiful changes the Lord has brought. Maybe you trust God more than yourself. Maybe you're more willing and faster to forgive. Maybe you crave time in the Word and are purposeful to follow its teachings. Do you see the fruits of the Spirit manifesting in your life? Have you lost those pesky, sinful desires, or are you at least seeing those desires wane?

Now ask God to show you where you're still hoarding habits of that old life. Let Him help you clear them out and instead fill your heart with His new way.

Dear Lord, help me be done with my old, worldly ways. Starting today, I want to fully embrace the beauty of this new life of faith in You. In Jesus' name, amen.

BE A PATTERN

Teach these things and make sure everyone learns them well.
Don't let anyone think little of you because you are young.
Be their ideal; let them follow the way you teach and live; be a pattern for them in your love, your faith, and your clean thoughts.

1 TIMOTHY 4:11–12 TLB

Paul is reminding Timothy that his age doesn't matter. Being young doesn't disqualify him. Instead, what counts is how he walks out his faith. It's how he shows love and communicates truth as he teaches. And notice that Paul is urging a steadfastness and consistency from this young man. He is telling Timothy to be a pattern for others. Friend, we too can embrace this calling in our lives today.

This world is quick to offer its own patterns for living, but ones filled with selfish desires, sinful cravings, and unhealthy habits. As believers, we are to establish godly patterns that are good for us and bring glory to God. And knowing others are watching us, the precedents we set matter even more.

So let's choose to love with great intention. Let's soak in God's presence so it spills out into every interaction with others. And let's monitor our words, thoughts, and actions, making sure they reflect our love for the Father. Let's create beautiful patterns, uncluttered by the worldly ones.

Dear Lord, teach me to live in ways that point all the glory to You in heaven. In Jesus' name, amen.

A CALM AND CONSIDERATE VOICE

As the Lord's slave, you shouldn't exhaust yourself in bickering; instead, be gentle—no matter who you are dealing with—ready and able to teach, tolerant without resentment, gently instructing those who stand up against you. Besides, the time may come when God grants them a change of heart so that they can arrive at the full knowledge of truth.

2 TIMOTHY 2:24–25 VOICE

We are to be gentle toward everyone, not quarrelsome. We're to be tolerant and patient without being offended, and kind in response to those who are mixed-up about what is right and good. And Paul tells us to be prepared to teach the truth. If we choose to be well mannered to those we encounter, there's a better chance they will, with God's prompting, declutter their lives of wrong ways of living and instead pursue righteousness.

Your interest in spiritual things probably wasn't piqued by people yelling about Jesus from the street corner. Hearing someone condemn your life choices or warn that you were on your way to hell probably didn't tender your heart either. Chances are it was a calm and considerate voice that opened your eyes to the truth of Jesus. Let's remember that.

Dear Lord, use me in the lives of others so they can find salvation through You. Remind me to share the gospel with a great measure of compassion and not condemnation. In Jesus' name, amen.

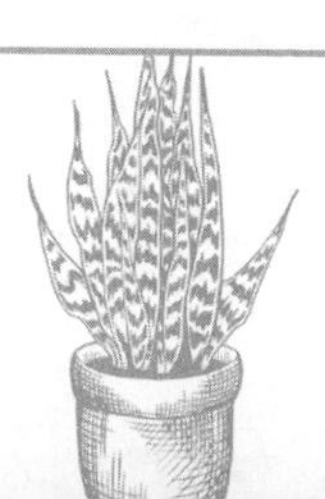

IT'S CHRIST

Christ himself is the Creator who made everything in heaven and earth, the things we can see and the things we can't; the spirit world with its kings and kingdoms, its rulers and authorities; all were made by Christ for his own use and glory. He was before all else began and it is his power that holds everything together.

COLOSSIANS 1:16–17 TLB

These two verses have power to clear out any fear or worry that's taking up precious space in your heart and usher in much-needed peace. Go ahead and reread them slowly, connecting with each word spoken aloud. Friend, did you need this beautiful reminder today?

What a gift to know that Christ is first and foremost. He is *the* Creator and designer. He puts people on the throne and takes them down. And He has made all things for His use and glory. The Lord is timeless. He is eternal and everlasting, without beginning or end. God is unchanging. Immutable. Even more, Christ is the one who holds everything together. . .not you.

So declutter your heart today through prayer. Lay down every situation that's robbing you of joy. Release the spine-weakening fear keeping you awake at night. And free yourself from anxious thoughts. Today, choose to rest in the truth that God is over all.

Dear Lord, what a relief to understand Your omnipotence and kingship over the heavens and the earth and everything in between. In Jesus' name, amen.

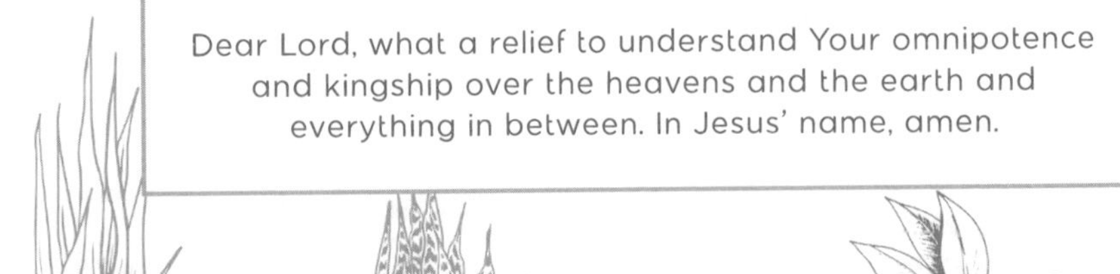

EMBRACING THE CALLING

Put these abilities to work; throw yourself into your tasks so that everyone may notice your improvement and progress. Keep a close watch on all you do and think. Stay true to what is right and God will bless you and use you to help others.

1 TIMOTHY 4:15–16 TLB

Like Timothy, if we invest in walking out the call God has placed on our lives, His goodness will be cultivated through us. If we're diligent to make the right choices, being confident they will delight God's heart, He will honor them. And staying true to His will and ways each day will not only bless you but also benefit others.

Friend, the Lord gave you unique talents and lovingly added them to your blueprints as He thought you up. He personally decided your giftings and where you'd use them. God even chose the exact time for you to come onto the kingdom calendar and bring those talents to light. Yes, you were made on purpose and for a purpose.

The world may try to push you down, crowd out your calling, or cancel you, but don't let anything stop your forward motion to embrace the plans God has appointed for you. Keep yourself full of faith and ready to do what is right and true.

Dear Lord, empower me to put my God-given abilities to work. I want my life to serve You in the meaningful ways You intended. In Jesus' name, amen.

GOD'S ECONOMY

"The more lowly your service to others, the greater you are. To be the greatest, be a servant. But those who think themselves great shall be disappointed and humbled; and those who humble themselves shall be exalted."

MATTHEW 23:11–12 TLB

God's economy is in the opposite direction of the world's economy. The more you get into the Word, the more you will see the reality of it. The world's way of doing things is driven by a particular set of rules and expectations, making it a bold choice to live God's way instead. Friend, it's not easy. The Lord knows this—which is why He promises to strengthen us, direct our steps, give us peace, and bless our obedience.

Where are you struggling to live God's way today? Knowing life clutters our hearts in all the wrong ways, what do you need to purge from yours? What keeps you from clearing these things out, making room for what God says matters most? As women who believe, we must make every effort to step forward in faith and live how the Lord instructs. It's only with His help that we'll be able to thrive in His economy.

Dear Lord, I confess that I often struggle to follow Your ways because they go against the ways of this world. And my sense of pride at times doesn't help either. Empower me to be confident and bold as I strive to embrace Your economy each day. In Jesus' name, amen.

WHAT MATTERS MOST

In this new life one's nationality or race or education or social position is unimportant; such things mean nothing. Whether a person has Christ is what matters, and he is equally available to all.

COLOSSIANS 3:11 TLB

Jesus matters most. Not the neighborhood you live in or the car you drive. Not the school your kids attend or the number of college degrees you have. Those luxurious vacations, that trendy wardrobe, and your home's stunning decor have no bearing on your eternal future. Whether you're black or white, rich or poor, American or Asian, blond or brunette, heavy or lean, tall or short, none of these labels matter. While they may mean something to us in the here and now, they are unimportant to God. And in today's verse, Paul is saying we should feel the same as He does. Whether a person has Christ is what matters, and He is equally available to all.

Let's not clutter our lives with mankind's hierarchy of importance. As believers, let's remember that our status here is fleeting and unfulfilling. Our priority should be putting our faith in Jesus and living in right relationship with the Lord. And as we do, others will be drawn to Christ and His goodness too.

Dear Lord, I don't want this world to have any hold on my heart. Help me to focus on You in all I do, because You matter most. In Jesus' name, amen.

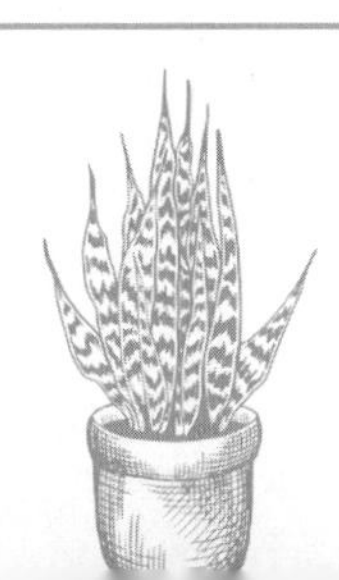

ORDER

Know your sheep by name; carefully attend to your flocks; (Don't take them for granted; possessions don't last forever, you know.) and then, when the crops are in and the harvest is stored in the barns, you can knit sweaters from lambs' wool, and sell your goats for a profit; there will be plenty of milk and meat to last your family through the winter.

PROVERBS 27:23–27 MSG

Everything has an order, and we have a responsibility to uphold order with wisdom and discernment. Remember that God doesn't create confusion or chaos in a believer. And for those who seek Him in earnest, He will consistently illuminate the right next step every time. He will never lead you astray.

So let the Lord lead you, friend. Whether you're navigating the ups and downs of relationships, bearing up under the heaviness of grief, discerning job opportunities, dealing with the emotions of estate planning or retirement, healing from hurts, or making life-altering choices, be quick to invite God into the process.

In this life, we often experience stress when we try to adhere to the world's fast pace of living. Everything starts to pile on top of us, clouding the way forward and crowding out peace and joy. But as we make room for God, He will settle our spirit and order our days according to His perfect plan.

Dear Lord, thank You for walking with me and offering peace in the process. In Jesus' name, amen.

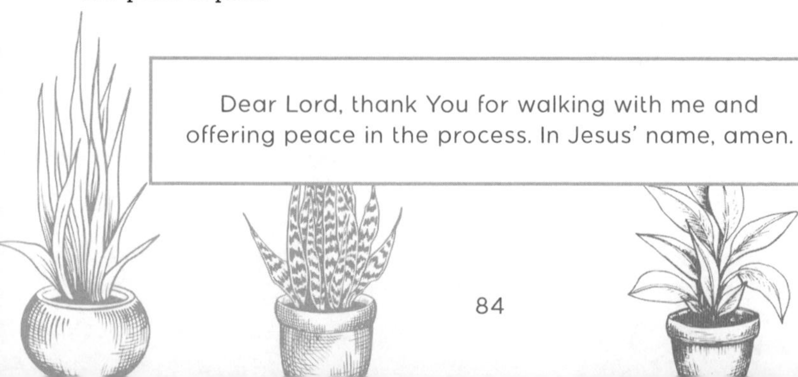

THE COMMAND TO LOVE

The most important commandment is this: "Hear, O Israel, the Eternal One is our God, and the Eternal One is the only God. You should love the Eternal, your God, with all your heart, with all your soul, with all your mind, and with all your strength." The second great commandment is this: "Love others in the same way you love yourself." There are no commandments more important than these.

MARK 12:29–31 VOICE

The command to love is the big one. And it's at the foundation of every relationship we have because it's essential to righteous living that pleases God. But how can we love Him with all our hearts, souls, minds, and strength when we're deeply rooted in the world's systems? How can we love others sacrificially when we're so focused on ourselves? The answer? We need the Lord to transform us from the inside out.

Every bit of time you spend soaking in God's Word allows the unhealthy habits to be replaced by godly ones. As you meditate on the Word, it penetrates your heart, renews your mind, restores your resolve, and reignites your purpose. The Bible reconnects you to the source of all things good and right, strengthening you to obey. And then the earthly thoughts littering your thinking are exchanged for the Eternal's love, enabling you to experience deep compassion.

Dear Lord, retrain me to love others as You have commanded. In Jesus' name, amen.

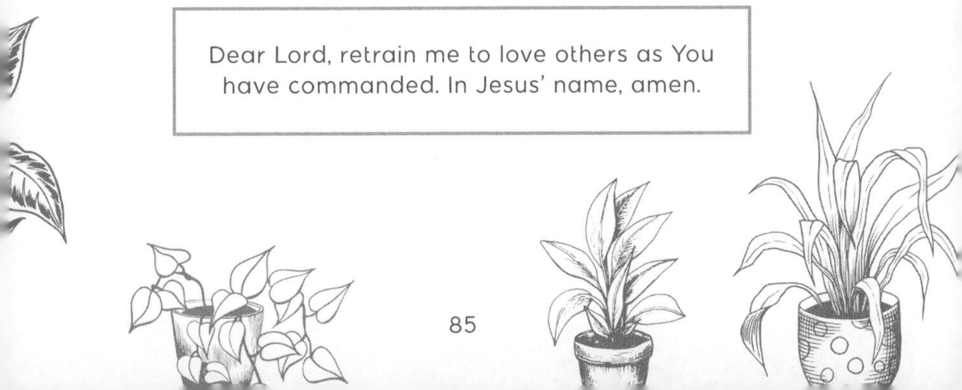

PRAYER IS A TOOL

So ever since we first heard about you we have kept on praying and asking God to help you understand what he wants you to do; asking him to make you wise about spiritual things; and asking that the way you live will always please the Lord and honor him, so that you will always be doing good, kind things for others, while all the time you are learning to know God better and better.

COLOSSIANS 1:9–10 TLB

In today's verses, Paul shares his petition to God regarding the Colossians. His prayer was for the knowledge and insight only God can give. He knew God would hear and answer.

The truth is that prayer is a powerful tool in the hands of a believer. It's a direct line of communication between you and God, available anytime and in every situation. Nothing is off limits. You can talk to God about your own struggles and the battles others are trying to navigate. You can share every worry, fear, or anxious thought. You can even pray liquid prayers without words because He has full knowledge of every detail weighing down your heart. What's more, prayer helps clean out what this world has cluttered. Spend time talking with God today.

Dear Lord, thank You for listening to me when I talk to You. Help me to remember that prayer is a powerful tool and a gift from You. In Jesus' name, amen.

CALLED TO LOVE OTHERS

Since you have been chosen by God who has given you this new kind of life, and because of his deep love and concern for you, you should practice tenderhearted mercy and kindness to others. Don't worry about making a good impression on them, but be ready to suffer quietly and patiently.

COLOSSIANS 3:12 TLB

What a beautiful truth to realize you've been chosen by God. You have been set apart and made holy. He is deeply involved in your life because He cares about you personally and loves you dearly. And it's because of these magnificent certainties that you can (and should!) practice compassion toward others. It's why you should show mercy and kindness whenever possible. And it's why God asks you to practice gentleness and patience with those around you. We each have a holy calling on our lives to love others well, following His example concerning us.

Life is hard enough these days, amen? It's getting harder to see good in a world quickly filling with godlessness. And all around us, people are struggling in so many ways. So let's take this command from Paul to heart, choosing to protect the unity of community and show compassion to one another. Who knows but that our care and concern will help others declutter their hearts and minds of the hard things and grab on to the hope of Jesus.

Dear Lord, May I be an encouragement to those around me. In Jesus' name, amen.

SERVING HIM WITH OUR LIFE

Then a poor widow came and dropped in two pennies. He called his disciples to him and remarked, "That poor widow has given more than all those rich men put together! For they gave a little of their extra fat, while she gave up her last penny."

MARK 12:42–44 TLB

This woman emptied herself, and Jesus took notice. He saw the immense sacrifice she made. He recognized the depth of her trust. And He knew her motives were pure. This woman's offering was a remarkable show of faith revealing that she was uncorrupted by worldly ways. Her heart was confident in the Lord's goodness, certain He would take care of her needs.

Is your conviction that strong? Do you believe the Lord will sustain you? Does He really bless obedience? Does God see you and hear your prayers, and will He show up when you need His help? Do you see a track record of His goodness in your life?

When we give everything we have to God, a supernatural exchange takes place. When we pour out our time or treasure, we're filled up with the assurance of His delight. A peace settles over us because we trust the Lord's sovereignty. And we recognize we're here to serve Him with our lives.

Dear Lord, give me the kind of faith that inspires daily service for You and Your kingdom. Give me opportunities that reveal my confidence in Your goodness, my certainty that You will always bless my obedience. In Jesus' name, amen.

THE LOVE OF MONEY

But people who long to be rich soon begin to do all kinds of wrong things to get money, things that hurt them and make them evil-minded and finally send them to hell itself. For the love of money is the first step toward all kinds of sin. Some people have even turned away from God because of their love for it, and as a result have pierced themselves with many sorrows.

1 TIMOTHY 6:9–10 TLB

The *love* of money has a way of exposing ugliness in each of us. It reveals our fleshly desires that are deeply rooted in the world. And for some, the pursuit of money causes us to compromise what we know is right to get it. Scripture says our worship of riches is the first step toward sin. The reality is that when greediness takes up space in our hearts, it pushes out godliness.

So how do we effectively keep ourselves decluttered from the love of money? First and foremost, let's remember that all good things come from God. Let's remember that we're to store up treasures in heaven, not here on earth. As we spend time in the Word and in prayer, these practices will make what we have. . .enough. Rather than pining for riches, we'll long for righteousness.

Dear Lord, while having money is not wrong, loving it more than You is. Help me to be content with what I have, keeping my priorities in order. In Jesus' name, amen.

QUICK TO FORGIVE

Be gentle and ready to forgive; never hold grudges.
Remember, the Lord forgave you, so you must forgive others.
Colossians 3:13 TLB

Few things can clutter a heart more than unforgiveness, because it tangles you up in knots, affecting every part of you. It keeps you holding on to offenses, justifying anger and bitterness toward others. The wrongdoing has a way of replaying in your mind, repeatedly and ad nauseam. And you end up talking about it with anyone who will listen. Left unchecked, it becomes almost an obsession.

But God commands us to forgive without fail. Forgiving others, however, doesn't mean we need to be doormats. Setting healthy boundaries is important. Just because we forgive someone doesn't excuse their behavior or suggest we weren't hurt. And our forgiveness doesn't let them off the hook. They'll answer to the Lord for what they've done. But choosing to extend grace to others honors the God who extended grace to us. And it keeps our hearts and minds free, focused on what is good and right.

Who is the Holy Spirit bringing to your mind right now? Where is unforgiveness cluttering your heart today? What offenses are you clinging to with all your might? Let God help you release those into His hands so you can be free.

Dear Lord, I confess all the places where I'm sitting in judgment and not forgiving. Please bring peace into my heart and help me to extend grace. In Jesus' name, amen.

THE NATURAL RESULT

If you find any comfort from being in the Anointed, if His love brings you some encouragement, if you experience true companionship with the Spirit, if His tenderness and mercy fill your heart; then, brothers and sisters, here is one thing that would complete my joy—come together as one in mind and spirit and purpose, sharing in the same love.

PHILIPPIANS 2:1–2 VOICE

Did you notice the four main ideas shared in today's verses and their anticipated outcome? Paul is trying to set expectations. He's saying that because of these four things. . .here is the natural conclusion. He doesn't want any worldly or personal clutter to get in the way.

These ideas are finding comfort in the Lord, being encouraged by Him, experiencing the Spirit's true companionship, and having a heart filled with His tenderness and mercy. So if these four things characterize our lives as believers, then as a community, we should naturally be one in mind, spirit, and purpose. A strong bond of love should knit us together.

Do you see these four things in your own life? Is any element lacking? Are you seeing the benefits with your family and friends? Being a believer is naturally a gift that keeps on giving, both to you and to those you love.

Dear Lord, let me be so saturated with Your love that I'm able to bless those around me in significant and meaningful ways. In Jesus' name, amen.

THE PRIVILEGE AND RESPONSIBILITY OF PEACE

Let the peace of heart that comes from Christ be always present in your hearts and lives, for this is your responsibility and privilege as members of his body. And always be thankful.

COLOSSIANS 3:15 TLB

If we are to let the peace of Jesus always be present in our hearts, then there's no room for fear or worry. But all too often our hearts are filled with anxious thoughts instead, effectively pushing out peace. The truth is that there simply isn't room for these two to coexist. Peace cannot thrive when fear has us stirred up. Friend, which one of these do you feel the most?

The unexplainable peace of God isn't only a privilege we experience as believers; it's also a responsibility. Consider that it takes focused intentionality to accept it from the Lord and ongoing nurture to keep it alive and active in our hearts. We must choose to reject fear and worry by laying them at the feet of Jesus. And then we must seek His peace, staying in that calming space with the Lord.

With His help, we can choose to ditch whatever causes us to be troubled and let Him bring comfort to our weary soul.

Dear Lord, I am desperate for the kind of peace that comes from You. The world may offer temporary relief, but Your peace is lasting and satisfies. In Jesus' name, amen.

THE BATTLE OF SELFISHNESS

Don't let selfishness and prideful agendas take over. Embrace true humility, and lift your heads to extend love to others. Get beyond yourselves and protecting your own interests; be sincere, and secure your neighbors' interests first. In other words, adopt the mind-set of Jesus the Anointed. Live with His attitude in your hearts.

PHILIPPIANS 2:3–5 VOICE

It's hard to be selfless in a world that promotes selfishness. And because humanity is inherently bent toward looking out for number one to begin with, we're fighting an uphill battle every day. We are self-centered in ways we don't even recognize. Friend, when our hearts are stuffed full of our wants, needs, and interests, not much space is left for loving others. We simply can't look past ourselves to see what those around us might need. We desperately need the Lord's help to get rid of this mindset and adopt His.

Ask God to reveal those places where you're self-seeking. Ask Him to uncover every prideful agenda where you're hoarding your own interests. Choose to surrender every tendency to control and manipulate in hopes of getting your way. Let Him fill you with love and compassion. And ask God to help you cultivate a kind, generous, and humble heart, always willing to put the needs of others first. It's impossible without Him.

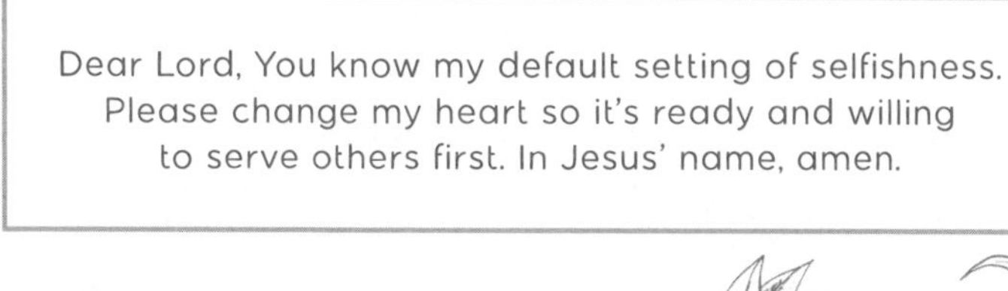

Dear Lord, You know my default setting of selfishness. Please change my heart so it's ready and willing to serve others first. In Jesus' name, amen.

SHINING LIGHT INTO DARKNESS

Do all things without complaining or bickering with each other, so you will be found innocent and blameless; you are God's children called to live without a single stain on your reputations among this perverted and crooked generation. Shine like stars across the land.

PHILIPPIANS 2:14–15 VOICE

As believers, we're to shine. It's through our words and actions that others will see Jesus in us. How we treat people really does make a difference, and as we show love and kindness, we point others to God. When our hearts are full of His goodness, it overflows into what we do and what we say.

Like today's verses mention, we are living among a perverted and crooked generation. Every form of evil is on full display for all to see. What's right is now considered wrong, just as what's wrong is embraced as right. And as we choose to live holy and righteous lives—not perfect, but purposeful—we will shine brightly together, bringing the Lord's light to combat this present darkness.

Let's spend concentrated and meaningful time in the Bible and in prayer so we're filled with faith and able to declutter our hearts of sin and selfishness so we can shine like stars. As God's children, sparkling with His holy light is our privilege and burden to bear.

Dear Lord, let my words and actions be securely rooted in You so I can effectively shine the light of Your goodness into the world. In Jesus' name, amen.

INHALING AND EXHALING

Remember what Christ taught, and let his words enrich your lives and make you wise; teach them to each other and sing them out in psalms and hymns and spiritual songs, singing to the Lord with thankful hearts.

COLOSSIANS 3:16 TLB

There are four calls to action in today's scripture. Four opportunities to stand firm in our faith through the ups and downs of life and encourage others to do the same. It's a beautiful cycle that starts with God and ends with Him too. And walking out this cycle with purpose and passion is how we keep our hearts so full of truth that nothing can push it out.

We're told to commit to mind the teachings of Jesus. We're to let them instill godly wisdom, the kind unmatched by the world. We're to be open and honest with others and freely share what we know about the Lord. And we are to sing the words of Christ back to God with thanksgiving, in whatever form that looks like to you. It's a call to inhale His goodness and exhale our gratitude.

Which of these feels hardest for you? Where are you excelling? What is the Holy Spirit showing you right now? Talk to the Lord about what's on your heart and then listen for His still, small voice.

Dear Lord, thank You for the Word and how it guides us into a deeper and more meaningful relationship with You. In Jesus' name, amen.

THE GIFT OF SPEAKING KINDLY

There is no one like Timothy. What sets him apart from others is his deep concern for you and your spiritual journey. This is rare, my friends, for most people only care about themselves, not about what is dear to the heart of Jesus the Anointed.

PHILIPPIANS 2:20–21 VOICE

What a gift that Paul spoke such kind words about Timothy. No doubt Paul's glowing report affirmed the validity of Timothy's ministry to others, especially coming from such a respected leader as Paul. But don't you imagine it brought much-needed encouragement to Timothy too? In a world that tries to beat you up almost every day, hearing appropriate and positive praise is most welcome.

Are you intentional about speaking highly of people? Do you offer accolades at the right time and in the right way? Is sharing your approval something you strive to do when it's fitting? The truth is that to many, our opinion as believers matters. Like Paul's did for Timothy, our timely endorsement can carry weight and help open doors.

Friend, we all become cluttered by negativity and mean-spiritedness from time to time. We all feel squeezed by the world's judgment in one way or another. Let's choose to be women who are quick to speak kindly to others and about others. Who knows what that kind of generosity could do for a weary and worried heart?

Dear Lord, let my words always be true and kind. In Jesus' name, amen.

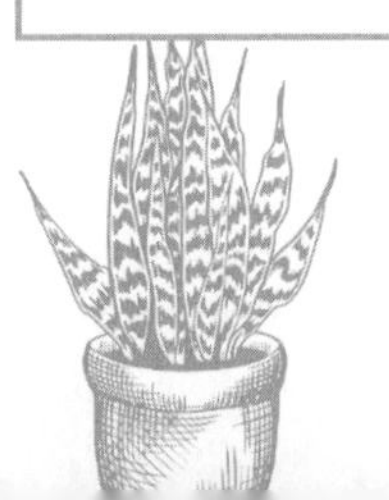

CLUTTERED WITH TRUTH

For us, there is one God, the Father who is the ultimate source of all things and the goal of our lives. And there is one Lord—Jesus the Anointed, the Liberating King; through Him all things were created, and by Him we are redeemed.

1 CORINTHIANS 8:6 VOICE

If you're going to clutter your life with anything, let it be filled to the brim with the truth from today's verse. We are women who believe that there is only one God, and He is our steadfast provider who gives us purpose. Whatever we need—be it physical, emotional, or spiritual—He will supply according to His perfect will and timing. And God's one and only Son, Jesus, created the heavens and the earth. It's through His death on the cross and resurrection that we are saved. There is no other way we can be redeemed and assured of an eternity in His presence.

Friend, be careful that no variation of this truth takes up space in your heart. Reject it swiftly. Don't be swayed by watered-down half truths designed to lead you astray. Don't entertain other opinions or ideas that question any part of the Bible. Add nothing, remove nothing, and tweak nothing. Stand strong in the truth written in God's Word. Lock it in your mind as you believe it with all your heart.

> Dear Lord, I believe in Your Word completely. Please sink its truths deep into my heart and mind. In Jesus' name, amen.

THE RIGHT FOUNDATION

"All who listen to my instructions and follow them are wise, like a man who builds his house on solid rock. Though the rain comes in torrents, and the floods rise and the storm winds beat against his house, it won't collapse, for it is built on rock."

MATTHEW 7:24–25 TLB

In this parable from Matthew 7, closing out the Sermon on the Mount, Jesus is asking those listening to decide if they'll follow the religious establishment of the day or His teachings. He is asking them to choose on which foundation they will build their lives moving forward. Will they live out the words of Jesus, proving themselves wise because their solid foundation as true believers will steady them through the hard times? Or will they continue with righteousness built on a sandy surface, which in the storms of life will quickly sink them and bring destruction?

When we fill our hearts with faith in Jesus and trust Him as our provider and protector, we're secure on solid rock. Strength comes from listening to His instruction *and* following it. It's important we do *both*. We may be shaken, but we won't collapse. The high winds will come, but God will steady us through them. And as we spend time in the Word and let its truths become the building blocks for the way we live, our faith will be mighty.

Dear Lord, please expose and remove any worldly foundation I'm trusting in. In Jesus' name, amen.

SEEKING GOD'S KNOWLEDGE ABOVE ALL ELSE

If anyone thinks he knows all the answers, he is just showing his ignorance. But the person who truly loves God is the one who is open to God's knowledge.

1 CORINTHIANS 8:2–3 TLB

If we were honest, we'd admit times we feel confident of our own wisdom. Maybe we've lived a lot of life and gained hard-won experience. Maybe we've gone far in education and are able to make sensible decisions. Maybe we've watched others and learned from the way they handled their own challenges. Or maybe we're well read and can pull insight from authors whose words speak to us. Yet while our hearts may be in a good place and our intentions noble, humanity severely limits our wisdom.

Today's verses tell us to seek God's knowledge above all else. We need Him to speak into our circumstances in meaningful ways. We need the Lord to fill us with *His* understanding so we don't lean on our own. And each day, our earnest prayer should be for God to open our eyes to His leading so we can follow with purpose and passion.

We may be very capable women, but His ways aren't our ways. The Lord's thoughts aren't our thoughts. And we need His input into every situation because of it.

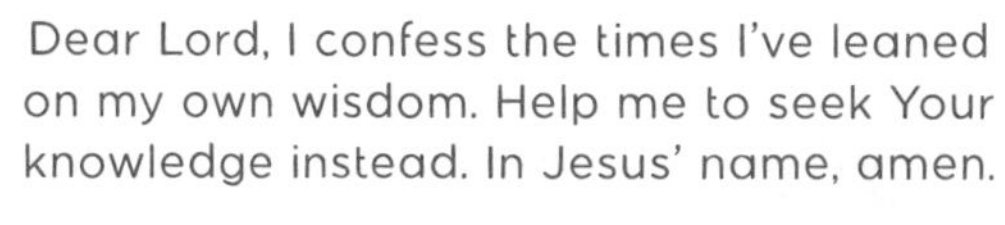

Dear Lord, I confess the times I've leaned on my own wisdom. Help me to seek Your knowledge instead. In Jesus' name, amen.

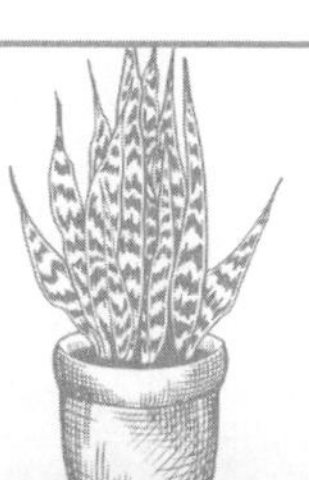

THE CLUTTER OF CRITICISM

"Stop judging so that you will not be judged. Otherwise, you will be judged by the same standard you use to judge others. The standards you use for others will be applied to you."

MATTHEW 7:1–2 GW

Today's scripture passage should catch your attention because it issues a serious warning. Simply put, we're not to declare someone guilty in punitive and severe ways. When we do, we'll be judged the same way by God. Take time to read the next few verses in this chapter to see that not all evaluation is prohibited, but harshness in opinion most certainly is.

Rather than look at someone's wrongs, let's stay focused on the journey we're walking out imperfectly each day. We shouldn't be preoccupied with the shortcomings and failures of those around us because we've also fallen short of God's glory. And sitting in judgment inevitably elevates us above them in our mind. Having critical and condemnatory eyes is sinful. Cluttering our hearts with disparaging thoughts displeases the Lord.

Friend, let God be God, recognizing He is the only one who can turn a life around. Instead of being hypercritical, let's pray for others with compassion. Let's recall our own seasons of sinning and cheer others on with understanding and humility. The truth is that we all need Jesus to remove ugly and ungodly words and actions and replace them with righteousness. Only He can do that.

Dear Lord, let my heart for others always be good. In Jesus' name, amen.

THE GREAT COMMISSION

Jesus, undeterred, went right ahead and gave his charge:
"God authorized and commanded me to commission you:
Go out and train everyone you meet, far and near, in this way
of life, marking them by baptism in the threefold name: Father,
Son, and Holy Spirit. Then instruct them in the practice of
all I have commanded you. I'll be with you as you do this,
day after day after day, right up to the end of the age."

MATTHEW 28:18–20 MSG

These words of Jesus are known as the Great Commission. His charge in these last verses of the last chapter of Matthew is the sending out of His disciples into the world by the authority of the Father. They were to introduce others to the gospel and train them to live in a right relationship with God. Jesus' ministry may have started in Israel, but His command was to share the good news with the world, both Jew and Gentile.

This is our instruction here and now too. In a world so packed with struggle and strife, many are weighed down with the bondage of it. What a privilege we have to tell them about Jesus, the one who can declutter those burdens and bring hope and freedom. Ask God to provide open doors of opportunity for you to share the good news with others. Be bold, friend.

Dear Lord, give me courage to share You with the world. In Jesus' name, amen.

SEEING OUR OWN WRONGS TOO

"So why do you see the piece of sawdust in another believer's eye and not notice the wooden beam in your own eye? How can you say to another believer, 'Let me take the piece of sawdust out of your eye,' when you have a beam in your own eye?"

MATTHEW 7:3–4 GW

Notice how Jesus uses carpenter-like terms here, possibly drawing on His experience in this line of work. Regardless, this is a powerful hyperbole that helps us understand something we may not be fully aware of. Friend, sometimes we spend so much time pointing out where others have fallen short without even recognizing where we do. We're busy pointing our finger at others without considering our own bad behavior. We sit in condemnation, being critical of those around us while somehow justifying our own sinfulness. It's ugly and wrong.

What if, instead, we asked God to reveal and heal our wrongs? What if we were aware of our sinfulness, humbled by our own iniquities, and also reached out to help others with genuine compassion? Rather than thinking of ourselves as better, what if we were able to relate and offered hard-won wisdom? What if we humbly shared our story and prayed for them and with them?

Judgment clutters our hearts and promotes sinful attitudes. Let's link arms with others and love through the hard times. . .*together*.

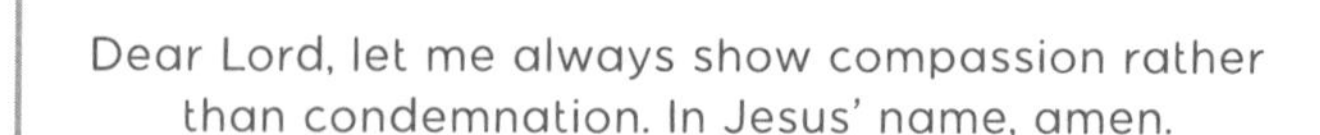

Dear Lord, let me always show compassion rather than condemnation. In Jesus' name, amen.

SHARING THE GOOD NEWS

Don't give precious things to dogs. Don't cast your pearls before swine. If you do, the pigs will trample the pearls with their little pigs' feet, and then they will turn back and attack you.

MATTHEW 7:6 VOICE

In Bible times and according to the Old Testament, Jews were to think of dogs and pigs as unclean. So in today's verse, these two are used to describe enemies of Israel. Pearls are considered to have great value, symbolizing the good news of Jesus. While believers are to be kind, compassionate, forgiving, and slow to judge, this scripture tells us to be wise as well. We're to have discernment to know when sharing the gospel with certain people is futile. Rather than continue trying to persuade, we're to move on to the next person.

While every soul is important to God, there are only so many ways we can present His goodness to someone set to reject it. The Holy Spirit in us will offer this nudge so we'll know when it's time to move on. And when we've been obedient to replace earthly thoughts with eternal ones, we can confidently release the individuals in our lives into God's hands.

Dear Lord, give me the strength to share the gospel with others and the discernment to know when they won't be receptive and it's time to move on. In Jesus' name, amen.

CHOOSING LIFE

I call heaven and earth as my witnesses against you right now: I have set life and death, blessing and curse before you. Now choose life—so that you and your descendants will live—by loving the L*ORD your God, by obeying his voice, and by clinging to him. That's how you will survive and live long on the fertile land the* L*ORD swore to give to your ancestors: to Abraham, Isaac, and Jacob.*

DEUTERONOMY 30:19–20 CEB

As Moses' life was coming to an end, he implored the Israelites to make a critical decision and choose life. This was an intentional determination to follow God each day—loving Him, obeying Him, and clinging to Him. Moses reminded them they had a choice to make, and it was key to receiving God's goodness and blessings. To choose life was to choose God.

We also must decide this for ourselves. To choose life means saying yes to Jesus as our personal Savior, ensuring that we'll spend eternity in His presence. It means emptying ourselves of selfish desires and asking to be filled with obedience to follow His will and ways instead. It's a call for our hearts to be saturated with love for the one we choose. . .every day.

Dear Lord, today and every day, I choose life. I choose You. Help me to love You, obey You, and cling to You as I navigate this world and until I see You face-to-face in eternity. In Jesus' name, amen.

A HUMBLE AND PERSISTENT HEART

Just ask and it will be given to you; seek after it and you will find. Continue to knock and the door will be opened for you. All who ask receive. Those who seek, find what they seek. And he who knocks, will have the door opened.

MATTHEW 7:7–8 VOICE

Today's verses reveal the very essence of prayer for the believer. Approaching God with a humble heart, faithful persistence, and steadfast confidence is key.

The beautiful promises tucked into this passage should encourage your heart today, friend. They should remind you that God sees you and loves you. He hears your pleas and petitions. His heart for you is always good. And as His child, you have the privilege of His presence as you come before Him.

Be confident that as you show perseverance in prayer, He will respond. As you seek the Lord, He will be found. When you ask for help, it will come according to His timing and will. And as you knock, God will open the door for you.

So be diligent to declutter any thoughts of God as a distant being who isn't available. The truth is, He's not only accessible but ready and willing to personally engage with you in meaningful ways.

Dear Lord, I appreciate the gift of prayer! Thank You for loving me and being there when I call out to You. Help me to be humble, persistent, and confident in You. In Jesus' name, amen.

VIRTUE SIGNALING

"Yes, woe upon you, Pharisees, and you other religious leaders—hypocrites! For you tithe down to the last mint leaf in your garden, but ignore the important things—justice and mercy and faith. Yes, you should tithe, but you shouldn't leave the more important things undone."

MATTHEW 23:23 TLB

According to the dictionary, a hypocrite is someone who puts on a false appearance of virtue or religion. They pretend to have morals and principles they don't possess. And the religious leaders in Bible times were prime examples, eventually exposed by Jesus Himself. Today, we'd call that virtue signaling. They strove to appear holy because they cared more for their status than their sanctification.

Let's be careful of how we live each day. As women of faith, let's be sure that who we are in private is also who we are in public. We can't be two faced and glorify God at the same time. Touting a phony faith to make us look better is blatant disobedience. We can't be one way in church circles and another in our private time. If we are, our eventual exposure as a poser may sway someone away from the Lord.

Ask God to authenticate your faith. Ask Him to remove the clutter of hypocrisy and virtue signaling. And as you soak in the Word and seek God through prayer, your faith will permeate every area of your life, both public and private.

Dear Lord, make me authentic. In Jesus' name, amen.

WHEN YOU NEED A FAITH BOOST

Jesus asked his father, "How long has he been like this?" The father replied, "He has been this way since he was a child. The demon has often thrown him into fire or into water to destroy him. If it's possible for you, put yourself in our place, and help us!" Jesus said to him, "As far as possibilities go, everything is possible for the person who believes." The child's father cried out at once, "I believe! Help my lack of faith."

MARK 9:21–24 GW

Isn't this father's faith precious? And what a relief to read his story in the Bible, realizing that even though we have accepted Jesus and believe in God's goodness, we often need a boost to help us trust more. This is something we all battle, friend. Even standing in the presence of Jesus wasn't enough for this dad, so he asked God for an extra measure of faith. We can do the same.

There are times when life just feels too big. We're struggling in our marriage or are trying to parent rebellious teenagers. Our health is failing, or our finances are a mess. Grief feels overwhelming, we're worried about the future, or we're caring for aging parents. In these moments, tell God that you believe but need Him to help your lack. Ask Him to fill you with faith that will drive out doubt. And watch it be so.

Dear Lord, help my lack of faith! In Jesus' name, amen.

CONFIDENT IN YOUR SALVATION

Oh, dear children, don't let anyone deceive you about this: if you are constantly doing what is good, it is because you are good, even as he is. . . . The person who has been born into God's family does not make a practice of sinning because now God's life is in him; so he can't keep on sinning, for this new life has been born into him and controls him—he has been born again.

1 JOHN 3:7, 9 TLB

Let this scripture challenge you to take an honest look at your life. Let it be a measuring stick, if you will, revealing the truth of your relationship with Jesus. It's a call to take inventory of the role sin plays and your desire for it. And if you'll let it be, it's also an affirmation for true believers.

Friend, if you are constantly doing what is good and rejecting sin-soaked opportunities, be confident in your salvation. If you want to follow God's ways more than your old ways, let your spirit be settled and stop questioning whether you're born again. The enemy loves to sow seeds of doubt in believers, keeping us from living in victory. So clear out the cluttered lies, embrace the truth of your faith, and stand in it securely.

Dear Lord, because I've asked Jesus into my heart and desire to do Your will above mine, I have confidence in my salvation. In Jesus' name, amen.

THE PATTERN OF GRACIOUS LOVE

If a person owns the kinds of things we need to make it in the world but refuses to share with those in need, is it even possible that God's love lives in him? My little children, don't just talk about love as an idea or a theory. Make it your true way of life, and live in the pattern of gracious love.

1 JOHN 3:17–18 VOICE

As believers, we should be generous with all we have. When God is truly in our hearts, we shouldn't want to hoard what He's blessed us with. Instead, we should want to give and share, because that's how we express His love toward others without prejudice.

But the truth is that loving this way is often hard to do. Sure, we can easily love people who are kind and gentle, those who treat us with thoughtfulness, and those who are quick to show gratitude. Certain people, however, make sharing sacrificially a difficult task to walk out because they're so rude, selfish, demanding, and curt. These kinds of people discourage our desire to show generosity.

Ask God to cultivate the pattern of gracious love within you so you're willing and able to pour out His love into a world that needs it.

Dear Lord, I want to love others in meaningful ways that bless them and bring glory to Your name. In Jesus' name, amen.

THE NEED FOR DISCERNMENT

Along the way, watch out for false prophets. They will come to you in sheep's clothing, but underneath that quaint and innocent wool, they are hungry wolves. But you will recognize them by their fruits. You don't find sweet, delicious grapes growing on thorny bushes, do you? You don't find delectable figs growing in the midst of prickly thistles.

MATTHEW 7:15–16 VOICE

We need to be so full of God's Word that we're able to discern right from wrong. Knowing what scripture says helps us understand the difference between what is false and what is true. And listening to the Holy Spirit through His gentle nudging will keep us following what's real rather than falling for what's fake.

Friend, are you committed to reading the Bible daily? Do you meditate on and memorize scripture, hiding it in your heart? Do you attend church in person or online and find encouragement through your pastor's sermon? Do you discuss your faith with a godly community, recognizing the Lord's footprints in your circumstances? It's through these things that we gain wisdom and discernment so we can accurately recognize false prophets and teachings.

In today's world, developing this kind of insight is essential. We may be living in the days of deception, but God has made a way for believers to stand strong against the wrong, the false, and the fake: continuously filling our hearts with His Word.

Dear Lord, help me to properly discern the times. In Jesus' name, amen.

MISINTERPRETATION OF SCRIPTURE

And Peter replied, "Each one of you must turn from sin, return to God, and be baptized in the name of Jesus Christ for the forgiveness of your sins; then you also shall receive this gift, the Holy Spirit. For Christ promised him to each one of you who has been called by the Lord our God, and to your children and even to those in distant lands!"

ACTS 2:38–39 TLB

Please don't hear what this passage of scripture is *not* saying. Peter is not implying that if you turn from your sins and return to God but are not baptized, then you won't be forgiven of trespasses and receive the gift of the Holy Spirit. The Bible never says that baptism is a condition or requirement of salvation. Instead, it's an outward sign of an inward decision to follow Jesus. The Word clearly states that we are saved by grace through faith in Jesus.

Sometimes scripture can be confusing and hard to understand. And if we don't take the time to dig into commentaries, ask a trusted friend or pastor, and pray for revelation, we may end up subscribing to bad theology. And that's dangerous because it may lead us astray.

Friend, ask God to reveal and remove clutter in your mind related to the misinterpretation of scripture. And be purposeful to research until you fully understand the truths contained in His Word.

Dear Lord, help me to know and understand the truths in the Bible without confusion. In Jesus' name, amen.

CONSTANT REMINDERS OF GUILT

There is a sure way for us to know that we belong to the truth. Even though our inner thoughts may condemn us with storms of guilt and constant reminders of our failures, we can know in our hearts that in His presence God Himself is greater than any accusation. He knows all things. My loved ones, if our hearts cannot condemn us, then we can stand with confidence before God.

1 JOHN 3:19–21 VOICE

Can you relate? Do your inner thoughts bring condemnation with storms of guilt? Are you constantly reminding yourself of every failure? Do your shortcomings have a way of scraping away at your confidence? Are your past bad choices or seasons of sinning still haunting you to this day? Let your faith replace that self-judgment, friend.

Whenever that inward condemnation harasses us, let's remember that God is bigger than any accusation. As believers, we've already been forgiven of those sins once and for all. They are covered by the blood of Jesus and His atoning work on the cross, and they no longer have power over us. We can purge them from our minds by praying for God's help to remind us of this powerful truth. And because He loves us so, He will remove our feelings of guilt and shame while bringing peace to our weary heart.

Dear Lord, I'm overwhelmed and worn out by self-condemnation. Please free me of it and comfort me with Your presence. In Jesus' name, amen.

AN INTENSE SENSE OF TOGETHERNESS

There was an intense sense of togetherness among all who believed; they shared all their material possessions in trust. They sold any possessions and goods that did not benefit the community and used the money to help everyone in need.

ACTS 2:44–45 VOICE

What a beautiful example of community. Rather than looking out for number one, the early Christians recognized that being stronger as a collective was best. Scripture says they experienced an "intense sense of togetherness" in which their hearts were supernaturally knit together, and they cared for one another with kindness and generosity. Rather than letting selfishness clutter their hearts, they chose to share everything and help everyone in need. How remarkable!

With God's help and a change in mindset, we also can live this way. We can create a community of friends and family who look out for each other, ready to stand in the gap when necessary. Our hearts can be knit together with compassion and care in a posture of sacrificial love. But unless we are purposeful to rid ourselves of greediness and discord and let God fill us with goodwill and harmony instead, it won't happen. It takes both our choice to surrender and the Lord's divine intervention to create an "intense sense of togetherness." Let's be the kind of women who focus on both.

Dear Lord, show me how to love better so I can experience togetherness with the people in my own life. In Jesus' name, amen.

ENVY AND JEALOUSY

What is causing the quarrels and fights among you? Isn't it because there is a whole army of evil desires within you? You want what you don't have, so you kill to get it. You long for what others have, and can't afford it, so you start a fight to take it away from them. And yet the reason you don't have what you want is that you don't ask God for it.

JAMES 4:1–2 TLB

The truth is that jealousy and envy are ugly realities for many of us. We struggle with coveting the worldly goods others may have that we don't. We hold on to bitterness with all our might. All too often a sense of resentment builds up in our hearts, even though we know better. We're fully aware of the warnings against envy found in the Bible, but sometimes we feel cheated and can't shake the sense of unfairness, however unwarranted it may be. Ultimately we end up acting out in ways that are unbecoming, and our sinfulness grieves the heart of God.

But what if we took our desires to the Lord in prayer and asked Him to sort them out? What if we confessed evil desires with humility and honesty? And what if we trusted that God knows all the desires of our hearts and will meet the ones in line with His will according to His plan and timing?

Dear Lord, help me to remember that I can take every need and want to You in prayer. In Jesus' name, amen.

THE NEED FOR DISCERNMENT

"Not all who sound religious are really godly people. They may refer to me as 'Lord,' but still won't get to heaven. For the decisive question is whether they obey my Father in heaven. At the Judgment many will tell me, 'Lord, Lord, we told others about you and used your name to cast out demons and to do many other great miracles.' But I will reply, 'You have never been mine. Go away, for your deeds are evil.' "

MATTHEW 7:21–23 TLB

This passage of scripture is sobering because it will be a harsh reality for many. Just speaking out the name of Jesus doesn't mean someone is repentant and saved by faith. Even doing good acts in Jesus' name may be meaningless if the person is really seeking their own fame over His. As believers, we must guard our hearts against the lure of these false prophets and disciples so we don't begin to follow them mindlessly.

Friend, the best way to guarantee our protection from this kind of blatant deception is by knowing what God's Word says. Unless we reject crafty half truths and fill up on correct full truths, how will we have the wisdom to know right from wrong and real from fake? Commit to spending time in the Bible daily so that the Lord can bring much-needed revelation and fortification.

Dear Lord, please open my eyes to every kind of deception so I don't become confused and reject truth. In Jesus' name, amen.

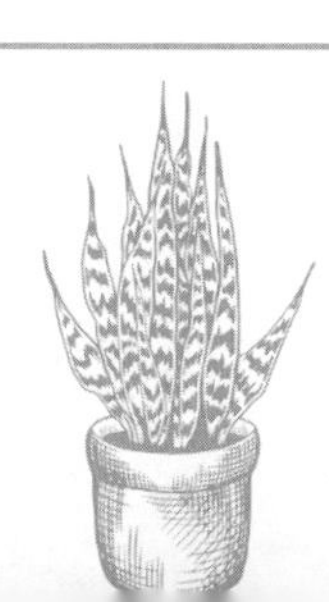

GIVING OURSELVES TO GOD

So give yourselves humbly to God. Resist the devil and he will flee from you. And when you draw close to God, God will draw close to you. Wash your hands, you sinners, and let your hearts be filled with God alone to make them pure and true to him.

JAMES 4:7–8 TLB

If we're to give ourselves humbly to God, we'll need to declutter our hearts, purging anything that keeps us from that beautiful surrender. What is that for you?

Are you overly focused on climbing the ladder of success, so it gets all your attention? Are your days filled with selfish desires, or even worthy ones, like working out, managing your home, or volunteering at your child's school? Are you struggling with jealousy and working hard to get what "she" has? Or are you trapped in a season of sinning, engaging in some kind of activity that has such a pull on your heart, it seems impossible to walk away from?

One of the devil's schemes is the art of distraction. He tries to get you focused on anything other than your faith, even if it seems like a wholesome choice. But anytime we clear out the eternal to make room for the earthly, it's sin. Friend, the only way believers can resist the devil so that he'll flee is to draw close to God.

Dear Lord, help me to understand how to give myself to You fully and completely so that the devil has no stronghold in my life. In Jesus' name, amen.

CONFIDENCE IN GOD

I will bless the Eternal, whose wise teaching orchestrates my days and centers my mind at night. He is ever present with me; at all times He goes before me. I will not live in fear or abandon my calling because He stands at my right hand.

PSALM 16:7–8 VOICE

In this psalm written by King David, you can feel his well-placed confidence oozing out. He's expressing his trust in God alone, standing steadfast because he knows the Lord will come through, just as He has time and time again. David isn't trusting in his own strength or another false god of the day. Instead, he is filled with an unwavering conviction of God's goodness. David writes these words with great certainty and assurance that should encourage us today.

The reality is that like this man after God's own heart, we will face hard times. It's inevitable, based on what the Bible tells us. We'll have to grapple with fear, anxiety, worry, grief, insecurities, and deep hurt. Various life storms will shake our foundation and unsettle our spirit. But as believers, we have the Lord on our side. And as we put our trust in Him, regardless of the circumstances we're facing, we can be confident that God will intervene in the right way and at the right time. We are secure in His hands. . .always.

Dear Lord, let my confidence be in You and Your dependable love. In Jesus' name, amen.

GOD'S LAW OF LOVE

Don't criticize and speak evil about each other, dear brothers. If you do, you will be fighting against God's law of loving one another, declaring it is wrong. But your job is not to decide whether this law is right or wrong, but to obey it. Only he who made the law can rightly judge among us. He alone decides to save us or destroy. So what right do you have to judge or criticize others?

JAMES 4:11–12 TLB

Unless we're intentional to love people according to God's law, falling into a pattern of judging others will come naturally. Scripture is crystal clear about this mandate. Loving your neighbors and enemies isn't a suggestion or option. But too often, we only acknowledge their shortcomings. We become hyperfocused on their failures because it makes us feel better about ourselves. Rather than showing grace, we point to places where they fall short and even share our uncharitable observations with others who might revel in them too.

Friend, when we act this way, we're fighting against God's rightful position as judge and ignoring His desire for us to invest in healthy community. Let's flush this disobedience from our hearts and ask Him to fill us with genuine compassion for others. If God commands us to love, then as believers, let's love well.

Dear Lord, I confess my critical and judgmental tendencies. Help me to choose to love instead, blessing others and obeying You. In Jesus' name, amen.

THE LORD IS THE SOURCE

You, Eternal One, are my sustenance and my life-giving cup. In that cup, You hold my future and my eternal riches. My home is surrounded in beauty; You have gifted me with abundance and a rich legacy.

Psalm 16:5–6 voice

The psalmist writes that God is his "sustenance" and "life-giving cup," meaning he recognizes the Lord to be the source of all joy and blessing. He is satisfied with who God is and what He has provided. The writer clearly doesn't feel the need to look to anything outside of God, because he views his inheritance from the Lord as more than enough.

Do you feel the same way? Rather than packing your life full of earthly treasures that cannot satisfy or sustain, do you find comfort in the abundance of what you already have as a believer? Is God enough in every way and in every circumstance? Or are you still running after money and reputation and what the world can offer? Are you looking for happiness in all the wrong places?

The reality is that nothing here on earth will ever match the powerful promises of God. They are weighty and true. He is irreplaceable, and there is no equal. And once we embrace this truth and live it out loud each day, the things of this world will grow strangely dim.

Dear Lord, I know You are my source and my portion and all I need. Thank You. In Jesus' name, amen.

GOD KNOWS OUR TOMORROW

How do you know what is going to happen tomorrow? For the length of your lives is as uncertain as the morning fog—now you see it; soon it is gone. What you ought to say is, "If the Lord wants us to, we shall live and do this or that." Otherwise you will be bragging about your own plans, and such self-confidence never pleases God.

JAMES 4:14–16 TLB

Friend, we're so full of ourselves sometimes! We set our own plans with many assumptions, often without asking God what His plans are. In our relationships, in our finances, in our careers, in our health, in our hopes and dreams, we walk forward without the Lord's guidance. We stand in our own wisdom and don't ask for His. We make judgment calls without divine discernment. And this self-confidence never pleases our heavenly Father.

Today's verses remind us that we have no idea what tomorrow holds, but our good and gracious God does. Making plans in and of itself isn't sinful. There's nothing wrong with planning out the week or month or year; it's necessary for functioning well. And working toward the future isn't bad either. But let's empty ourselves of blatant self-reliance and instead make plans prayerfully, trusting that God's perfect plan will always come to light.

Dear Lord, thank You for knowing my tomorrow so I can trust You today. Let my plans always be trumped by Yours. In Jesus' name, amen.

EVEN WHEN LIFE IS GOOD

This is a good life—my heart is glad, my soul is full of joy, and my body is at rest. Who could want for more? You will not abandon me to experience death and the grave or leave me to rot alone. Instead, You direct me on the path that leads to a beautiful life. As I walk with You, the pleasures are never-ending, and I know true joy and contentment.

PSALM 16:9–11 VOICE

Friend, even when our life is full of gladness, joy, and calm, we still need the Lord. Sometimes when we're in that sweet spot where everything is humming along without incident, we tend to ignore God. Not necessarily in a conscious or dismissive way, but when our hearts aren't weary or in need of His intervention, we don't feel desperate. We're not crying out for help or hope. And we go it alone, enjoying the sweetness of the moment. But the truth is that we always need the Lord, be it in a season of peace or a season of problems.

Be careful not to squeeze God out when life is easy. Don't shelve time in the Word or in prayer when things seem good. Be the kind of woman who embraces her faith with the same passion no matter what. Let others see how you navigate the ups and downs of life, both the challenges and the celebrations.

Dear Lord, You are important in every season of life. In Jesus' name, amen.

DECLUTTERING SINFUL BEHAVIOR

Don't you know that people who are unjust won't inherit God's kingdom? Don't be deceived. Those who are sexually immoral, those who worship false gods, adulterers, both participants in same-sex intercourse, thieves, the greedy, drunks, abusive people, and swindlers won't inherit God's kingdom. That is what some of you used to be! But you were washed clean, you were made holy to God, and you were made right with God in the name of the Lord Jesus Christ and in the Spirit of our God.

1 Corinthians 6:9–11 CEB

Let today's verses strengthen your resolve to keep your life decluttered from sinful thoughts and activities. There is simply no room in your life for these things. While we're imperfect people living in an imperfect world, we can't let that reality make us lazy. It's not an excuse or a justification for bad behavior.

Because we're believers, we've been washed clean from our old ways. Jesus' blood made us holy when we accepted Him as our personal Savior. He made us right with God the Father. And as His children, we have the daily privilege and burden of pursuing the things of the Lord and turning away from every wicked thing. We're to devote our lives to the cultivation of holiness.

Dear Lord, help me to keep my eyes on the prize of eternity with You. May my life always bring You glory. In Jesus' name, amen.

PRAYER FOR OUR LEADERS

You have loved what is right and hated what is wrong.
That is why God, your God, has anointed you, rather
than your companions, with the oil of joy.

PSALM 45:7 GW

This psalm is about the celebration of a God-fearing king who puts a premium on being just and fair. Throughout his reign, he is one who seeks truth. He loves what God loves and hates what God hates. He carries out initiatives that directly benefit the nation rather than himself, desiring to secure the health and prosperity of his people. And God delights in him.

The Bible clearly tells us to pray for those in authority so they'll choose to lead with peace and bring blessings on the people. We should be actively asking God to prick the hearts of our leaders so they come to resemble the king described here, praying that their time in office will bring goodness and hope to future generations. But instead, many of us merely grumble about our leaders. We complain and let hopelessness take root. Our hearts are cluttered with judgment rather than earnest petitions to the Lord. And we forget that Daniel 2:21 (GW) says, "He removes kings and establishes them."

Let's commit to praying for those God chooses to put in command. We can confidently trust that God is in control, working out all things for our good and His glory.

Dear Lord, I trust You even when I don't fully understand all the things You do. In Jesus' name, amen.

AFFECTING GENERATIONS

Do not make an idol for yourself—no form whatsoever—of anything in the sky above or on the earth below or in the waters under the earth. Do not bow down to them or worship them, because I, the Lord *your God, am a passionate God. I punish children for their parents' sins even to the third and fourth generations of those who hate me. But I am loyal and gracious to the thousandth generation of those who love me and keep my commandments.*

Exodus 20:4–6 CEB

Friend, our genuine faith in Jesus has the power to affect generations to come. God says He will be loyal and gracious to those who come behind us for thousands of years if we will love Him and follow His commands now. Do we recognize the gift we're giving our families by being full of Jesus rather than being full of the world?

Let this be the encouragement you need to remove those sinful habits and ungodly idols from your life. If you are prioritizing any earthly things before the eternal God, have the courage to oust them today. Ask for His help! And if there's anyone or anything you go to for comfort rather than the Lord, repent and refocus. Remember that your faith, whether anchored here or in heaven, will affect generations to come.

Dear Lord, help me to worship You above all else so my faith blesses the future. In Jesus' name, amen.

DEPENDING ON GOD

Dear brothers, warn those who are lazy, comfort those who are frightened, take tender care of those who are weak, and be patient with everyone. See that no one pays back evil for evil, but always try to do good to each other and to everyone else. Always be joyful. Always keep on praying. No matter what happens, always be thankful, for this is God's will for you who belong to Christ Jesus.

1 THESSALONIANS 5:14–18 TLB

The Bible is clear about how we're to live each day. It tells us how to love others and love the Lord in meaningful and practical ways. It teaches us about kindness. It tells us when to speak up and warn others. It tells us when to show comfort and care. It reminds us to show gratitude, even when it feels counterintuitive to our circumstances. It exhorts us to show great patience to everyone around us. And honestly, heeding all these admonishments sometimes feels impossible.

But if we saturate our spirits in His Word, ask God to meet us in our lack, and let the overflow of His goodness spill into the lives of others, then we will be a blessing to those around us, and God will be pleased. As the Lord fills us with His strength, we are able.

Dear Lord, You ask me to live in ways I can only accomplish with Your help. I'm beginning to understand that's by design! Help me to depend on You. In Jesus' name, amen.

THE BEAUTY OF MENTORSHIP

This is my last gift to you, this example of a way of life: a life of hard work, a life of helping the weak, a life that echoes every day those words of Jesus our King, who said, "It is more blessed to give than to receive."

ACTS 20:35 VOICE

The apostle Paul wrote today's verse knowing from that point forward, his life would be full of persecution, hardship, and imprisonment. With this letter to the church in Ephesus, he's releasing them into God's hands but also giving them marching orders. Paul offers final instructions for living in ways that will please the Lord. And he's trying to shape their mindset and encourage them in the faith, as this is his last goodbye.

There is something so sweet about being mentored by those who love God and have our best in mind. Paul deeply loved believers and poured out his godly wisdom to empower them for Christian living. Do you have a mentor? Are you a mentor to someone?

Jesus said it is "more blessed to give than to receive," so let's unpack our hard-won wisdom, formed through God's goodness, with those around us. Let's model what godly living looks like, even in our imperfection. We have walked through the ups and downs of life with the Lord and have a testimony to share.

Dear Lord, give me opportunities to speak truth and encouragement to others, and I will do so! In Jesus' name, amen.

SETTING OURSELVES APART

Don't be naive. There are difficult times ahead. As the end approaches, people are going to be self-absorbed, money-hungry, self-promoting, stuck-up, profane, contemptuous of parents, crude, coarse, dog-eat-dog, unbending, slanderers, impulsively wild, savage, cynical, treacherous, ruthless, bloated windbags, addicted to lust, and allergic to God. They'll make a show of religion, but behind the scenes they're animals. Stay clear of these people.

2 TIMOTHY 3:1–5 MSG

Friend, Jesus is coming back soon! While we don't know the day or hour, that doesn't negate the call to prepare ourselves. Difficult times are here—and here to stay. We're going to be met with all forms of evil. And the need to navigate unimaginable hardship will be inescapable. . .it probably already is. But according to the Word, Jesus is coming for His church, and we can rest with confidence in that truth and be at peace. . .always.

Until then, we are to set ourselves apart from the kind of people listed in today's verses. It's not that we're sitting in judgment and condemnation, because that would be sinful. Instead, we're decluttering ourselves of negative influences that may pull us away from righteous living. This is wisdom. This is prudence. This is following God's Word.

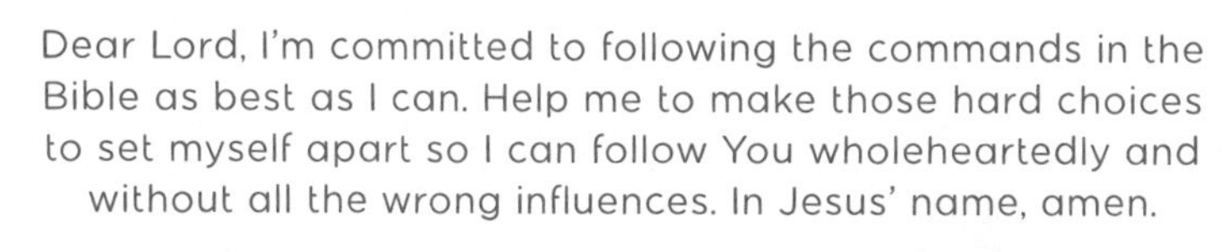

Dear Lord, I'm committed to following the commands in the Bible as best as I can. Help me to make those hard choices to set myself apart so I can follow You wholeheartedly and without all the wrong influences. In Jesus' name, amen.

WISDOM RATHER THAN WEALTH

"Prefer my life-disciplines over chasing after money, and God-knowledge over a lucrative career. For Wisdom is better than all the trappings of wealth; nothing you could wish for holds a candle to her."

PROVERBS 8:10–11 MSG

The pursuit of happiness almost always includes the pursuit of wealth. And because happiness is based on our circumstances, when we're struggling financially, we're often filled with gloom and grief. When we can't seem to earn enough money to keep up with others, we feel miserable. And when we overspend and are in the red with no relief in sight, unhappiness clutters our hearts. This is why our greatest pursuit should be chasing after the eternal God and His wisdom—not earthly wealth and its trappings.

The life of a believer is marked by joy in the Lord, which is based not on circumstances but on Christ. The goal is to collect God-knowledge so that we can thrive in a right relationship with the Lord, following His will and ways rather than seeking our own selfish desires. We need His wisdom to navigate a world littered with substitutes for genuine joy.

Today's scripture is spot-on when it says that nothing here can hold a candle to heavenly things. Regardless of worldly offerings, always be intentional to seek God's goodness and blessings.

Dear Lord, help me to seek Your wisdom above all things. Everything I truly need is in You. In Jesus' name, amen.

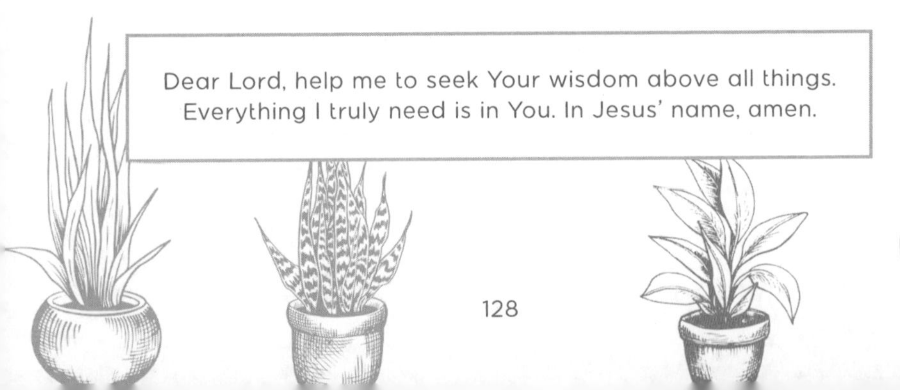

THE GIFT OF THE BIBLE

The whole Bible was given to us by inspiration from God and is useful to teach us what is true and to make us realize what is wrong in our lives; it straightens us out and helps us do what is right. It is God's way of making us well prepared at every point, fully equipped to do good to everyone.

2 TIMOTHY 3:16–17 TLB

Many of us may not fully understand what a gift the Bible is to a believer. We may not realize it's the key to living a righteous life that pleases God. We may overlook its necessity to saturate our hearts with truth that then flows into every area of our lives. And we may not understand the power of God's Word to declutter our hearts of all the wrong things. So if we're not spending quality time sitting with the scriptures daily, we're missing out on one of His greatest blessings.

Friend, let the Bible teach you the difference between right and wrong, good and bad. Let it point you in the right direction when you're at a crossroads. Let the Word prepare you for what's ahead as well as equip you to navigate the journey well. Let it provide you with hope and help.

Dear Lord, thank You for the gift of Your Word. I'm committed to digging into it each day. In Jesus' name, amen.

WHICH MASTER DO WE SERVE?

You've made your choice. Your ambition is to look good in front of other people, not God. But God sees through to your hearts. He values things differently from you. The goals you and your peers are reaching for God detests.

LUKE 16:15 VOICE

In today's verse, Jesus was calling out the Pharisees for mocking Him. He'd been talking to the crowd about the impossibility of serving two masters, both God and money, and how every believer needed to make a choice to follow one or the other. Through His teaching that day, the Pharisees' love of money had been exposed publicly, and they were angry. These leaders worked to look good in front of the common folk, but the Lord knew their hearts were in a different place. Their values didn't line up with what they preached or what God commanded. And in the way only Jesus can do, He revealed their hypocrisy with precision.

This same concept applies to us today. With each decision and choice, we are serving either money or our Maker. Our hearts are set on earthly treasures or on the ones stored up in heaven. We strive to either impress or bless. There's only room for one in our hearts, and the other must go.

Dear Lord, since I must choose this day whom I will serve, I choose You! Help me to fill my life in ways that bring You glory. In Jesus' name, amen.

CLUTTERING LIFE WITH THE USELESS

So I became greater than any of the kings in Jerusalem before me, and with it all I remained clear-eyed, so that I could evaluate all these things. Anything I wanted I took and did not restrain myself from any joy. I even found great pleasure in hard work. This pleasure was, indeed, my only reward for all my labors. But as I looked at everything I had tried, it was all so useless, a chasing of the wind, and there was nothing really worthwhile anywhere.

ECCLESIASTES 2:9–11 TLB

In today's scripture passage, the writer (often referred to as the Preacher, since Ecclesiastes was penned anonymously) shares how he had achieved great things. He became greater than other kings. He fully embraced anything that might bring joy to his heart. He worked hard and deeply enjoyed it. And he determined this pleasure was his reward. But in the end, as he took inventory, he realized all the things he had done were worthless.

Let's learn from this powerful section of scripture as we navigate each day. The truth is that so much of our life is chasing the wind. We get hyperfocused on the wrong things and cling to them with all our might. But cluttering our life with the useless only leaves us empty. Instead, let's go all in with our faith and build a beautiful relationship with God, walking out the plan created for us before we took our first breath.

Dear Lord, You are my pursuit and purpose. In Jesus' name, amen.

THE RIGHT STUFF

How thankful I am to Christ Jesus our Lord for choosing me as one of his messengers, and giving me the strength to be faithful to him, even though I used to scoff at the name of Christ. I hunted down his people, harming them in every way I could. But God had mercy on me because I didn't know what I was doing, for I didn't know Christ at that time. Oh, how kind our Lord was, for he showed me how to trust him and become full of the love of Christ Jesus.

1 TIMOTHY 1:12–14 TLB

Before God changed his name to Paul, he was known as Saul. This man was a lawyer and part of the Sanhedrin, the Jewish supreme court, and he was uncompromising about his faith. Because of his religious extremism, Paul hunted down Christians and had them killed. In his mind, he was doing the right thing by ridding the world of them. Then he had a Damascus Road encounter with Jesus that changed everything.

Paul had filled his days doing what he thought was right in the eyes of God. But, wow, was he wrong! Friend, we can fall into the same trap. Ask the Lord to reveal where you've gotten it wrong so you can fill your days with the right stuff instead. Ask Him to confirm or change your focus.

Dear Lord, I trust You to redirect me if needed. I'm listening. In Jesus' name, amen.

GOD DIRECTS OUR STEPS

If you are right with God, He strengthens you for the journey; the Eternal will be pleased with your life. And even though you trip up, you will not fall on your face because He holds you by the hand.

PSALM 37:23–24 VOICE

When today's scripture passage says God will strengthen you for the journey, it means He will be with you, guiding your steps as you seek His direction. If you're a believer, He'll make certain your steps are solid ones. And whether they're small steps that seem insignificant or giant steps way out of your comfort zone, God cares about them all. What a relief to know He won't leave us to figure things out alone. He's pleased with our life of purpose and promises to catch us when we stumble.

These are the kinds of verses that help declutter our hearts of fear. They help remove worry and anxiety because we can be confident of the truth that God is holding our hand, right now and always.

So, friend, what is your current journey? Are you fighting for your marriage or trying another procedure to get pregnant? Are you digging your way out of debt or trying to shine Jesus into your workplace? Are you trying to overcome an addiction or muster the courage to share your testimony? Rest, knowing God is with you and will guide each step forward.

Dear Lord, I trust You. In Jesus' name, amen.

THE PROMISE OF BLESSING

"May the Lord bless and protect you; may the Lord's face radiate with joy because of you; may he be gracious to you, show you his favor, and give you his peace."
NUMBERS 6:24–26 TLB

God told Moses to have Aaron and his sons speak these words over the people of Israel as a special blessing. It was to be considered a promise that He would personally bless them in meaningful and significant ways. Imagine the comfort these words brought to each person who heard them. Friend, we can be encouraged and comforted today too.

If you're a believer, this promise includes you. Without fail, you can know that God will bless and protect you each day. You can believe that you bring Him joy, simply because you exist. You can trust in the Lord's goodness, kindness, and generosity and be confident His favor will shine down on your life. And you can expect His perfect peace to remove any chaos and confusion, settling your spirit and calming your heart.

If you truly believed God could love you in such ways, how would such a belief declutter those feelings of worthlessness that often overwhelm you? How would it remove the offenses that replay in your mind? Spend time with the Lord today, repenting where necessary and asking for hope.

Dear Lord, help me to be confident in the promise of Your blessing. In Jesus' name, amen.

WHEN OUR HEARTS' DESIRES CHANGE

Believe in the Eternal, and do what is good—live in the land He provides; roam, and rest in God's faithfulness. Take great joy in the Eternal! His gifts are coming, and they are all your heart desires!

PSALM 37:3–4 VOICE

Written by King David, this psalm encourages us to invest in our relationship with God. How do we do that? We're to believe in Him, rest in His faithfulness, and find joy in His companionship. This is important! Because when life's storms come, we'll be able to trust God more easily as we purpose to do what is good. And as we do, blessings will come—the ones that will delight our hearts.

But here's what cultivating a strong relationship with the Lord will also do: What used to bring happiness won't any longer. Those sinful and fleshly desires will be supernaturally removed, and our hearts will begin to long for things like peace, patience, kindness, grace, mercy, and self-control. The cravings for worldly treasures will be replaced with the pursuit of godly ones. And as our faith matures, we'll naturally start to love what God loves and hate what He hates. Our hearts will align with His more and more, and we'll seek His will over ours. Just watch.

Dear Lord, help me to invest in my relationship with You through time in the Word and in prayer so my desires begin to align with Your plans for my life. In Jesus' name, amen.

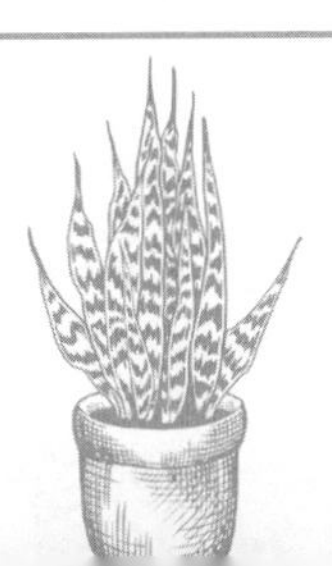

YOU'RE FULLY AND COMPLETELY LOVED

The Lord said to me, "I knew you before you were formed within your mother's womb; before you were born I sanctified you and appointed you as my spokesman to the world."

JEREMIAH 1:4–5 TLB

How incredible to realize that before Jeremiah was created, God knew him. Before he was conceived and grew in his mother's womb, the Lord was fully aware of every detail of his life. Before Jeremiah even took his first breath or first step, God had complete knowledge of this man and his purpose. He was sanctified and appointed as the Father's spokesman to the world before the world was formed. This is mind blowing.

So, friend, if God identified this prophet before his time, we can rest assured He knew us too. He thought us up in advance, designing with great intention who we would be and what we would do. He chose our skill sets and the ways in which we'd contribute to the body of believers. God even decided when we'd come onto the kingdom calendar.

Let this powerful truth demolish any lies that say you're unloved and unworthy. Remember, the one who spoke the heavens and earth into existence knows you and loves you without condition.

Dear Lord, I'm humbled to realize how much I'm valued by You. I understand now that I matter and have great importance in Your eyes. Help me to remember this truth every day. In Jesus' name, amen.

THE PROBLEM WITH SELF-RELIANCE

Commit your path to the Eternal; let Him direct you. Put your confidence in Him, and He will follow through with you. He will spread out righteousness for you as a sunrise spreads radiance over the land; He will deliver justice for you into the light of the high sun.

PSALM 37:5–6 VOICE

Self-reliance will always get us in trouble, especially as believers. We're simply not meant to navigate life on our own. While the world may preach the concept of being independent and taking care of ourselves, God's plan for humanity is in the opposite direction. The world says we should find our own resources for living, but as those who follow the Lord, we know that He is our great provider in every way.

What the psalmist suggests here is revolutionary and beautiful. It's a reminder that God is ready, willing, and committed to be part of our lives. We can have confidence in His goodness, certain it will be for our good and His glory. And God's presence will always be with us until we see Him face-to-face.

Let's clear out every bit of prideful self-reliance from our hearts and minds and recognize our need for the Lord. With His help, we are capable of so many things. And He will empower us in every way, every day.

Dear Lord, I've lived dependent on me, rather than You, too often. Help me to trust You first and foremost. In Jesus' name, amen.

THE VALUE OF WISDOM

For the value of wisdom is far above rubies; nothing can be compared with it. Wisdom and good judgment live together, for wisdom knows where to discover knowledge and understanding. If anyone respects and fears God, he will hate evil. For wisdom hates pride, arrogance, corruption, and deceit of every kind.

PROVERBS 8:11–13 TLB

Let's make sure we're not storing pride, arrogance, or any form of corruption in our hearts. Today's verses tell us that God hates these things because they're evil in His eyes. And they go against the godly wisdom believers can access through Him. All we have to do is ask through prayer and then wait for the Lord to show us the way forward. His guidance may be immediate, or it may come slowly. But once we sense His leading, we should pray for confirmation. Remember that God cannot and will not contradict Himself, so make sure what you're sensing as His voice always aligns with the Word.

If we're diligent to live out of His wisdom, what we'll store in our hearts instead will be a supernaturally inspired knowledge and understanding that are priceless. This wisdom is valued even more than rubies! Nothing in this world compares to it! And our commitment to seek the Lord's discernment will reveal the fullness of our faith in Him and our unmatched fear of Him.

Dear Lord, show me the way forward! I am waiting to hear from You. In Jesus' name, amen.

GOD NOTICES

Day by day the Lord observes the good deeds done by godly men, and gives them eternal rewards. He cares for them when times are hard; even in famine, they will have enough. But evil men shall perish. These enemies of God will wither like grass and disappear like smoke.

PSALM 37:18–20 TLB

God notices. Each time you err on the side of faith, it's noted. When you're quick to forgive, love the unlovable, and stop gossip in its tracks, He sees it. It takes confidence to go against groupthink and stand strong for the Lord. It's hard to follow His ways when yours feel easier. Being patient, having self-control, showing kindness, and giving generously all take intentionality. Seeking God by spending time in the Word and talking to Him in prayer is a choice. But be assured that He never misses your faith in action.

Friend, the Bible confirms that the Lord sees every single decision you make and deed you do. What's more, He promises that He will care and provide for you when hard times come and you find yourself lacking.

Let this powerful truth fill your heart today, pushing out any doubt or fear that's occupying it now. Be encouraged to continue living a righteous life. . .even when you think no one notices. Because He always does.

Dear Lord, thank You for seeing me and blessing my obedience. Let my life always bring You glory. In Jesus' name, amen.

EXPOSING OUR HUMANITY

"I love all who love me. Those who search for me shall surely find me. Unending riches, honor, justice, and righteousness are mine to distribute. My gifts are better than the purest gold or sterling silver! My paths are those of justice and right. Those who love and follow me are indeed wealthy. I fill their treasuries."

PROVERBS 8:17–21 TLB

God is reminding us that His gifts are better than anything the world can offer. Even those resources and items we consider valuable here cannot match what the Lord provides to those who love and seek Him. So it would make sense that trying to store up earthly riches rather than eternal ones is a waste of time, talent, and treasure.

Scriptures like these expose our humanity. Our minds simply cannot grasp all that God is and does. We cannot fully understand the blessings our obedience ushers in. We're too busy trying to make a name for ourselves here to realize that we're completely known in the heavens. And we decide earthly wealth should be our greatest gain.

Ask God to fill your heart with truth today. He is your source for all things, and when your eyes are on Him, everything else falls into place according to His will. You are known. You are loved. And your faith in the Lord brings the wealth that truly matters.

Dear Lord, help me to trust in You more than earthly gains or goods. In Jesus' name, amen.

BECAUSE GOD IS MY SHEPHERD

Because the Lord is my Shepherd, I have everything I need! He lets me rest in the meadow grass and leads me beside the quiet streams. He gives me new strength. He helps me do what honors him the most. Even when walking through the dark valley of death I will not be afraid, for you are close beside me, guarding, guiding all the way.

PSALM 23:1–4 TLB

Why did the psalmist feel content? Why was he able to trust that his needs would be met? Why could he rest and have his strength renewed? He tells us why in the first sentence: it's because he recognized the Lord as his shepherd.

Sometimes we look to all the wrong things for help. We clutter our hearts with short-term fixes and insufficient options. What about you, friend? Who or what do you depend on for peace? Maybe you trust in your husband or parents. Maybe you're dependent on the medical community or slick politicians. Maybe you find comfort in movie or television show binges or retail therapy. Or maybe you've dabbled in another religion or false god.

Waste no time in purging yourself of wrongly placed hopes and unrealistic expectations. Repent of filling up on anything other than God. And from today forward, let the Lord be your only shepherd.

Dear Lord, thank You for being my provider in every way, all the time, and no matter what. In Jesus' name, amen.

THE BLESSING OF WISDOM

"Happy is the man who is so anxious to be with me that he watches for me daily at my gates, or waits for me outside my home! For whoever finds me finds life and wins approval from the Lord."

PROVERBS 8:34–35 TLB

In this proverb, wisdom is represented by a woman who's calling out to those passing by, offering nuggets of truth to each of them. Take time to read the entire chapter for a stronger understanding of godly wisdom and its rich blessings for believers. But today, let's recognize how it allows us to find life and receive favor from the Lord.

Without God to guide us through the ups and downs of life, we'll find ourselves cluttered by self-reliance and worldly ideas. Each troubling circumstance should cause us to eagerly seek His wisdom. Every difficult conversation, big decision, confusing moment, challenging relationship, or worrisome situation needs divine intervention. And as we soak in the truths of His Word and pray with fervor, God will show us the way. We'll gain insight and direction, as well as blessings that flow from obedience.

Let's be women who go to the Lord when wisdom is needed. Rather than run to our bestie, let's start with prayer first. God will always guide us through with skilled precision.

Dear Lord, there is life in Your wisdom and favor from seeking it. Thank You for both! May I run to You before looking to anyone or anything else. In Jesus' name, amen.

YOUR WISDOM OR HIS?

When the greedy want more, they stir up trouble;
but when a person trusts in the Eternal, he's sure to
prosper. Anyone who puts confidence only in himself is a fool,
but the person who follows wisdom will be kept safe.

PROVERBS 28:25–26 VOICE

The choice is between our wisdom and God's. It's deciding if we should move forward based on what we know or seek the Lord to guide us. It's resting in our limited and shortsighted discernment or trusting in the one who has full and complete knowledge of the situation. Friend, do you feel comfortable with your partial understanding, or might it make better sense to pray in earnest and wait for God to show you the next right step?

As women, we're expected to make hundreds of quick decisions each day. Between managing our homes, supporting the needs of our family, and engaging in our work, taking time to pray may seem silly. Life moves at a quick pace! But what if we started each morning in prayer, asking the Lord to fill our hearts and minds with His wisdom for each decision we face? Let's be intentional to replace the world's ways with the Lord's plans. Let's show faith in action, trusting God to put us on the best path.

Dear Lord, I want Your wisdom every day. I need Your discernment to replace any worldly ideas that cross my mind. In Jesus' name, amen.

GOD KNOWS YOUR MOTIVES

People go about making their plans, but the Eternal has the final word. Even when you think you have good intentions, He knows your real motives. Whatever you do, do it as service to Him, and He will guarantee your success.

PROVERBS 16:1–3 VOICE

Every day, we find ourselves making plans, which is fine and good. In fact, making plans is important since we're often the glue that holds the family together. We may be the designated friend who organizes get-togethers. Unless we set things in motion, the workflow may stop dead in its tracks. We're usually the party planners, chore setters, carpoolers, and social directors. And while we may think our intentions are pure, God's Word reminds us that He knows what is really behind those plans. He knows if they're motivated by fear, bitterness, or worry.

Let's ask Him to declutter our hearts of anything that causes us to plan with wrong intentions, even if we're not aware of it. Let's choose to depend on the Lord to confirm or change our plans according to His will. We can trust He'll bless good plans and bring them to fruition in the right ways and at the right time. And as we seek to glorify God in all we do, our motives will align with His majesty and success will follow.

Dear Lord, I know You see the motives behind my plans, and I trust that You will help me to keep them pure and honoring. In Jesus' name, amen.

SUFFERINGS

If we are God's children, that means we are His heirs along with the Anointed, set to inherit everything that is His. If we share His sufferings, we know that we will ultimately share in His glory. Now I'm sure of this: the sufferings we endure now are not even worth comparing to the glory that is coming and will be revealed in us.

Romans 8:17–18 voice

Friend, taking inventory of our sufferings can be humbling. They may include the loss of someone we deeply loved. Or a painful discovery of betrayal that led to an unwanted divorce. Or maybe a child who faced trauma that led them down the wrong path. Or grief over the death of a dream we never got to experience. Or legal trouble that brought financial ruin. Or the challenges of trying to blend families in a new marriage. Or a diagnosis that feels hopeless. We've collected a lifetime of sufferings, hoarding them in our hearts often without meaning to. And we've lost perspective.

Paul refocuses us in today's scripture when he says that what we've had to endure pales in comparison to the glory of what's coming. Let this beautiful truth trump the hardships that life has brought. When we see Jesus and experience eternal life with Him, we won't give our suffering here another thought.

Dear Lord, I needed to read this today. Thank You for well-placed reminders of heaven. In Jesus' name, amen.

THE HELPER

The Father is sending a great Helper, the Holy Spirit, in My name to teach you everything and to remind you of all I have said to you. My peace is the legacy I leave to you. I don't give gifts like those of this world. Do not let your heart be troubled or fearful.

JOHN 14:26–27 VOICE

The Holy Spirit is a gift every believer receives when they accept Jesus as their personal Savior. He lives within them, growing them and guiding them as their faith matures. He imparts and inspires. He coaches and challenges. The Spirit brings revelations and reminders. And He provides peace and power. The Father always takes care of those who love Him in ways that reveal His goodness. We never have to walk through this life alone.

If you let Him, God's Spirit will push out the bad habits and hang-ups the world has installed. The fear that stirs you up every day and keeps you awake at night will be replaced by faith as the Spirit strengthens your trust muscle, effectively squeezing out worry and anxiety. Nothing here can come close to competing with God's good gifts.

Dear Lord, I confess that I've tried to navigate this life by myself and failed. My heart has been cluttered by heartbreak and stress, and I'm overwhelmed. Thank You for the Holy Spirit. Thank You for knowing I'd need peace in this life. In Jesus' name, amen.

FOR YOUR GOOD AND HIS GLORY

We are confident that God is able to orchestrate everything to work toward something good and beautiful when we love Him and accept His invitation to live according to His plan.

Romans 8:28 voice

As believers, we can trust with certainty that God works all things together for good. No matter what you're facing right now, the Lord is working in it. Be it the details surrounding a death, a divorce, a deception, or a debt, His hands are currently involved. You can be confident God is laboring toward something beautiful that is for your good and His glory. Friend, we can *know* this!

Yet knowing God is working in our situation doesn't mean it will feel good at the time. Nor does it mean we'll get everything we desire. God's ways and thoughts are not our ways and thoughts. But He can see the big picture and knows the ins and outs of our circumstances. And in His great sovereignty, the Lord will orchestrate things so His plan for us comes to pass. It won't be thwarted, because we were created on purpose and for a purpose.

Take a minute to thank God for His love and willingness to be involved in your life in such significant ways. Tell Him you love Him and trust His plans. And ask for help to walk them out daily.

Dear Lord, You are the leader of my life and I trust You. In Jesus' name, amen.

GIVING GOD YOUR WORRIES AND FEARS

If you will humble yourselves under the mighty hand of God, in his good time he will lift you up. Let him have all your worries and cares, for he is always thinking about you and watching everything that concerns you.

1 PETER 5:6–7 TLB

The Lord is offering to take from you all that stirs your spirit and keeps you anxious. What a beautiful invitation to purge your heart from every worry and fear that clutters it each day. Scripture says that God thinks about you continually. Friend, did you know that you're always on His mind? He sees you and is fully aware of all that causes concern and weighs you down.

But it takes humility to give these things up. We often decide to hang on to our burdens for a variety of reasons. Maybe we think God doesn't care or they're too insignificant for His intervention. Maybe we think we'll handle them best. Or maybe shame or guilt is attached, and we'd rather stay silent about them. Look back at today's verses and let the Word replace the lies with God's truth.

There's no good reason to try to fix our lives alone. God never intended us to navigate the bumpy roads without Him. Spend time in prayer today, unpacking each worry and fear and laying them at His feet. Feel His comfort fill the empty spaces. Feel His peace settle in your heart.

Dear Lord, here are my worries and fears. . . . In Jesus' name, amen.

NO CONDEMNATION IN CHRIST

Therefore, now no condemnation awaits those who are living in Jesus the Anointed, the Liberating King, because when you live in the Anointed One, Jesus, a new law takes effect. The law of the Spirit of life breathes into you and liberates you from the law of sin and death.

ROMANS 8:1–2 VOICE

What a relief to know that as believers forgiven of our sins, we no longer face condemnation. Jesus' death on the cross secured our complete forgiveness. As He hung there, every one of our sins—past, present, and future—hung with Him. Jesus took the punishment for our trespasses, paying the price to free us from the sin that condemned us. And His sacrifice isn't conditional—no one and nothing can separate us from His love. We are forever secure in Christ.

Your enemy, the devil, knows this too. And because he cannot undo your salvation, he goes to work, filling your heart with feelings of unworthiness. He floods you with fault for failures and shame for shortcomings. He heaps blame and piles on memories of times you fell short. And before long you forget that because of Jesus, you're liberated from this guilty verdict.

Friend, you are fully forgiven. That means as a believer, you have a new law in effect, breathed into your life by God Himself, clearing out every bit of condemnation. You are free, so remember to live that way.

Dear Lord, thank You. Thank You! In Jesus' name, amen.

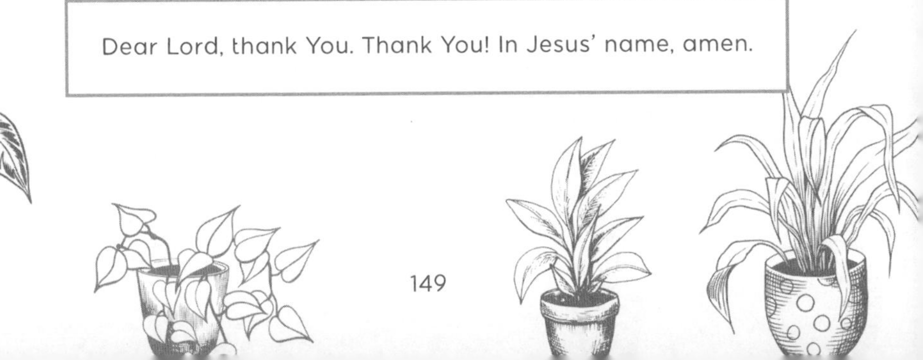

WHEN THE ATTACKS COME

Be careful—watch out for attacks from Satan, your great enemy. He prowls around like a hungry, roaring lion, looking for some victim to tear apart. Stand firm when he attacks. Trust the Lord; and remember that other Christians all around the world are going through these sufferings too.

1 PETER 5:8–9 TLB

What Satan really wants to do is personally hurt God, but he understands it's impossible. He has no power or authority over the Father whatsoever. So instead, he goes after His children, hoping to grieve God's heart. Today's scripture passage warns us of this truth, saying Satan prowls the earth looking for someone to attack. He is our greatest enemy and always looks for ways to steal from us, kill us, and destroy us. So we're told to stand firm in faith when these attacks come, realizing we're not alone.

Ask God to fill you with His strength and wisdom to know how to navigate the enemy's assaults. Be diligent to spend time in the Word daily, and let the truths found in its pages drive out doubt and create confidence. Talk to the Lord. When you feel chaos pushing away your peace, cry out for His help. Ask for His eternal perspective. And remember there are other believers experiencing the same attacks, so you're in good and godly company.

Dear Lord, help me to stand firm in You when the attacks come. I know You will give me all I need. In Jesus' name, amen.

THE FLESH OR THE SPIRIT?

If you live your life animated by the flesh—namely, your fallen, corrupt nature—then your mind is focused on the matters of the flesh. But if you live your life animated by the Spirit—namely, God's indwelling presence—then your focus is on the work of the Spirit. A mind focused on the flesh is doomed to death, but a mind focused on the Spirit will find full life and complete peace.

Romans 8:5–6 voice

Every day, we get to choose how we're going to walk out our waking hours. We'll be led either by our flesh or by the Spirit. And while the choice may be simple on paper, it's difficult to carry out in our thoughts and actions. Those fleshly desires come easily because they're in our nature. We're born sinful into a sinful world. So unless we choose to put our faith in the Lord, our flesh will rule the day.

Paul is calling us higher. In today's verses, he's revealing the tension we navigate as humans. And he reminds us that a saving faith in Jesus changes everything. Depending on what we focus on, we'll be full of either chaos or peace. Our eternity will be in hell or heaven. And if we choose correctly—although we may walk it out imperfectly—our hearts and minds won't be cluttered with worthless works but we'll live full lives saturated with God's goodness.

Dear Lord, I choose You. In Jesus' name, amen.

SUFFERING ISN'T FOREVER

After you have suffered for a little while, the God of all grace, the one who called you into his eternal glory in Christ Jesus, will himself restore, empower, strengthen, and establish you. To him be power forever and always. Amen.

1 PETER 5:10–11 CEB

The gold nugget takeaway from this passage of scripture is knowing that suffering isn't forever, friend. It may feel that way at times, but this heartbreaking season will come to an end, and God will bring restoration. He'll empower you to purge the pain and find hope again. You will be strengthened for forward motion full of passion and purpose. And God will personally establish you once more, helping you find your footing with healthy expectations.

The Bible clearly tells us we will experience peace-draining and spine-weakening moments here on earth. But before they have the chance to enter our lives, God must approve or deny them. And remember that He only allows suffering for our good and His glory, and only for a little while. That means we can trust Him in it and through it to the other side. It also means we don't suffer for nothing. Because of His sovereignty, we can trust there is always great purpose, even if we struggle to see it in the moment.

Dear Lord, keep my heart free from anger or blame toward You for my suffering. I choose to trust You fully. In Jesus' name, amen.

THE SPIRIT WILL ARTICULATE

A similar thing happens when we pray. We are weak and do not know how to pray, so the Spirit steps in and articulates prayers for us with groaning too profound for words. Don't you know that He who pursues and explores the human heart intimately knows the Spirit's mind because He pleads to God for His saints to align their lives with the will of God?

ROMANS 8:26–27 VOICE

What a gift to know that when we're at a loss for words and can't seem to speak our prayers concisely or with clarity, the Holy Spirit intervenes. Every time life punches us in the gut and we're left speechless, He articulates for us. And in our weakness, when we have no idea how or what to pray, His Spirit steps in on our behalf. The Father knows there are times when life is messy and we can't declutter our minds, so He made a way.

God has blessed each believer with the Holy Spirit as our constant companion. He is our guide. He is the one who spurs us into action, nurturing the desire to align our lives with God's will. So every time we feel unable to pray with purpose and passion, we can be fully confident the Spirit understands us and will effectively connect our hearts to God's heart.

Dear Lord, You always think of everything, and I'm so very grateful. In Jesus' name, amen.

STRENGTH AND BOLDNESS

I want to remind you to stir into flame the strength and boldness that is in you, that entered into you when I laid my hands upon your head and blessed you. For the Holy Spirit, God's gift, does not want you to be afraid of people, but to be wise and strong, and to love them and enjoy being with them.

2 TIMOTHY 1:6–7 TLB

Paul penned this very personal letter to his young protégé from a jail cell. He knew his execution was around the corner and wanted to encourage Timothy to stand strong in faith, protect the gospel message, and share the path of salvation. Paul's death would require Timothy to lead the church, which was a huge responsibility for this young man. And Paul wanted to ensure that Timothy's gifts would remain strong, bold, and effective.

Paul didn't want anything to hinder Timothy's calling to preach, because he knew full well the ways that intimidation tends to crowd out purpose. With deep love and affection, Paul reminded Timothy that the Holy Spirit would empower him with strength and boldness.

Be encouraged, friend. Don't let anything replace the divine purpose God has placed in your heart. Ask Him to protect it so it remains unaffected by clutter and chaos. Trust Him for strength to do what you've been called to do. And ask for a beautiful boldness to say what needs to be said.

Dear Lord, I know You will protect the purpose You've placed in my heart. In Jesus' name, amen.

GOD'S LOVE IS UNWAVERING

But no matter what comes, we will always taste victory through Him who loved us. For I have every confidence that nothing—not death, life, heavenly messengers, dark spirits, the present, the future, spiritual powers, height, depth, nor any created thing—can come between us and the love of God revealed in the Anointed, Jesus our Lord.

ROMANS 8:37–39 VOICE

God's love is unwavering. It's unshakable. And nothing on earth or in heaven—or in between—has the power to undo it. His love is secure and stable and cannot be revoked in any way, ever. You can be fully confident that regardless of how often you mess up, you are His forever. Friend, there's nothing you can do to make the Lord love you any more or any less than He does right now.

Whatever lies are cluttering your heart today—especially the ones saying you're unlovable—ask God to purge them. Ask Him to remove the untruths whispering into your spirit that you're unworthy of His goodness. If you ask, the Lord will oust every falsehood that's filling your thoughts and robbing you of peace. These kinds of lies are designed to bring hopelessness and render us ineffective for the kingdom. Don't put up with them a second longer.

Dear Lord, remind me that Your love is irrevocable and that I can never lose it no matter how many mistakes I make. In Jesus' name, amen.

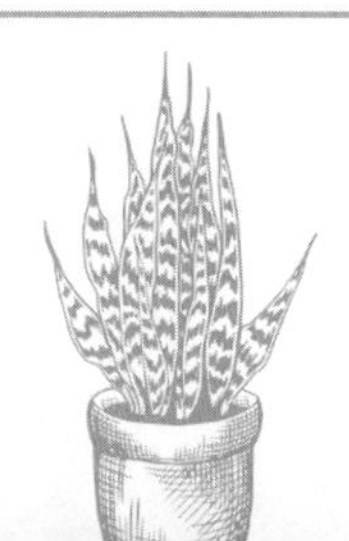

DON'T PANIC

"Don't panic. I'm with you. There's no need to fear for I'm your God. I'll give you strength. I'll help you. I'll hold you steady, keep a firm grip on you."

ISAIAH 41:10 MSG

What are the things filling you with fear today? Are you battling a disease that feels overwhelming? Have you lost a friendship you thought would last forever? Has another month passed without a positive pregnancy test? Is your marriage on divorce's doorstep and you're out of ideas? Is your debt out of control and you can't seem to dig out from under it? Are you in a season of sin and drowning in shame? Is your child walking a path of destruction and can't see the truth?

Sweet friend, don't panic, because God is with you. You are deeply loved, and He sees what's happening. The Lord understands why you're scared and reminds you of the power of His presence. He promises to strengthen you to stand strong. He promises to help you and steady you against the worry and angst threatening to squeeze out your peace. The Father is with you, holding you through every knee-wobbling fear at play. You're never alone.

Reread today's verse out loud and ask God to help you believe it by faith. Let the truths unpacked in Isaiah help replace your fear with His comfort.

Dear Lord, today I can barely stand under the weight of fear. Please help me. In Jesus' name, amen.

THE CHOICE TO BE STILL

"Be still, be calm, see, and understand I am the True God. I am honored among all the nations. I am honored over all the earth."

PSALM 46:10 VOICE

Sometimes the best thing we can do is be still. But as there's so much chaos in the world today, simply being still is a tall order.

Being intentional to just stop can help bring a sense of calm to our hearts. In these prayerful moments, we're able to gain a fresh perspective on the situation. This doesn't necessarily mean we have to stop moving about our day. For many, that's almost impossible with a home to run, a family to support, or deadlines to meet at work. But we can be still in our spirit and wait for God to meet us there. We can remember our position in regard to His, understanding the Lord to be sovereign and in control. We can choose to rest in Him, trusting that we're seen, that our situation is known. . .and that He's at work.

Be careful not to partner with anything that unsettles you. Be quick to pray and ask for God's peace and wisdom. And ask Him to help keep your mind from the clutter that leads to fear and worry.

Dear Lord, remind me to be still when my heart starts to race with worry. Help me to stand strong in the truth that You are the true God, honored and holy. In Jesus' name, amen.

SURE AND FEARLESS

No fear, no pacing, no biting fingernails. When the earth spins out of control, we are sure and fearless. When mountains crumble and the waters run wild, we are sure and fearless. Even in heavy winds and huge waves, or as mountains shake, we are sure and fearless.

PSALM 46:2–3 VOICE

No matter what happens today, the Lord is with you. He will strengthen you to face whatever is coming tomorrow. And the enemy's plans for chaos in the weeks and months ahead are no match for God's power in you through faith. The Word says we will face hard times in this life, but they won't conquer us. Even though the world may seem crazy, the unthinkable may happen, and storms may blow through, we can be sure and fearless.

Let's stop letting these challenges clutter our thoughts and ruin our days. As believers who spend time in God's Word regularly, we know they will come. We will have to navigate moments and seasons that feel scary—it's a fact. But also, as believers, we can know with confidence that the Lord is present and active in those circumstances. He will stay close and equip us for victory. God will always help us through.

Dear Lord, I struggle to be strong, sure, and fearless when I'm facing heartachingly difficult situations. Help me to trust You so that I can rest and find comfort. In Jesus' name, amen.

UNHINDERED FELLOWSHIP

I heard a loud voice from the throne say, "God lives with humans! God will make his home with them, and they will be his people. God himself will be with them and be their God. He will wipe every tear from their eyes. There won't be any more death. There won't be any grief, crying, or pain, because the first things have disappeared."

REVELATION 21:3–4 GW

Soon we will experience unhindered fellowship in the presence of the Lord. We will be together with our Creator in the new Jerusalem that will descend from the heavens. He will make all things new, and our everyday lives will be purged of all that plagues us today. God will reverse the curse that sin brought into the world.

There will be no reason for tears. Nothing will break our hearts or usher in sadness. There will be no death or the grief it ushers in. We won't battle infertility or navigate the pain of miscarriage. There will be no brokenness through divorce or the discovery of infidelity. Our thoughts won't be cluttered by fear, worry, or anxiety. Friend, as believers, let's remember that this earth is not our home, and this life is but a breath. And there will come a day—hopefully soon—when we'll enjoy unhindered and unending fellowship with the Lord.

Dear Lord, thank You that life here isn't lasting. I look forward to being with You in a new way, every day, forever. In Jesus' name, amen.

FROM THE HEART

Whatever you do, do it from the heart for the Lord and not for people. You know that you will receive an inheritance as a reward. You serve the Lord Christ.

COLOSSIANS 3:23–24 CEB

When we do something "from the heart for the Lord," what does that mean? Well, let's remember what it *doesn't* mean first. We're not doing something to meet God's needs, because He has no needs. He is self-sufficient and enjoys fellowship within the Trinity. And even more, there is nothing He can't do! What it *does* mean is found at the end of today's passage.

When we obey the Lord because we want to grow closer to Him and delight His heart, He blesses us. Serving with a humble heart brings its own reward. It's not a matter of giving God what He needs but rather a matter of creating a way for Him to give us what we need. And serving "from the heart for the Lord" also keeps our motives in check, ensuring that we're doing things not to impress but to bless. Our focus is kingdom work.

Remember, the Lord's economy is vastly different from the world's. Let's be diligent to fill our hearts with genuine obedience and pure motives because we want all God has to offer.

Dear Lord, I confess the times I've served for the wrong reasons. Help me to live out this passage from Colossians today and every day. In Jesus' name, amen.

SET FREE TO LIVE FREE

Christ has set us free to live a free life. So take your stand!
Never again let anyone put a harness of slavery on you.
GALATIANS 5:1 MSG

Because of Jesus' perfect sacrifice on the cross, we've been set free from the oppression of the Mosaic law and the sin that cluttered our life, keeping us enslaved in unhealthy ways. But many of us forget this powerful truth.

Today's verse is part of the letter Paul wrote to the Galatians, reminding them of this freedom. False teachers were infiltrating their churches and preaching legalism, saying believers must return to Old Testament laws and ceremonies. These teachers essentially told the Galatian believers to reject their freedom in Christ and replace it with the bondage of rules that no longer applied. This was bad teaching!

Friend, if you're a believer in Jesus Christ as the Son of God and have accepted Him as your Lord and Savior, then you have been set free. His blood spilled on the cross covers you today. And that means you're free from any condemnation. You're free from the power and penalty of sin and the old laws. And while this freedom doesn't permit you to continue sinning, it instead empowers you to live a holy and pleasing life. It emboldens you to love others through the Spirit's leading. And it enables you to follow God's will and thrive.

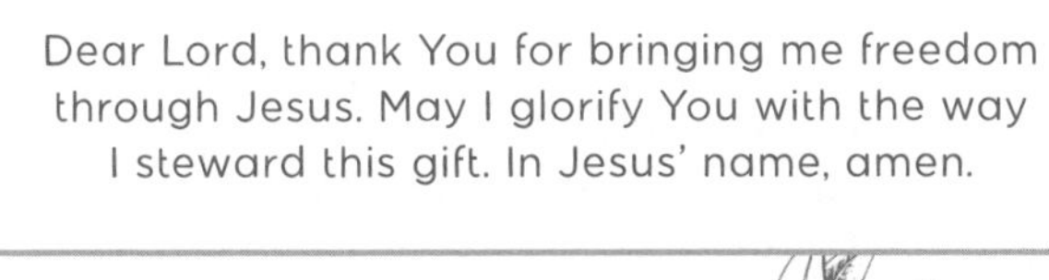

Dear Lord, thank You for bringing me freedom through Jesus. May I glorify You with the way I steward this gift. In Jesus' name, amen.

RECOGNIZING GOD AS CREATOR

In the beginning, God created everything: the heavens above and the earth below. Here's what happened: At first the earth lacked shape and was totally empty, and a dark fog draped over the deep while God's spirit-wind hovered over the surface of the empty waters. Then there was the voice of God.

GENESIS 1:1–2 VOICE

If God created everything from nothing, speaking into existence heaven and earth and all in between, why do we struggle to trust Him with our challenging circumstances? What keeps us from falling into His arms when life is overwhelming? And why do we regularly put our faith in worldly remedies or our own strength when the storms blow in?

Until we choose to embrace our amazing God and all the blessings that come from being believers, living holy and pleasing lives for Him, our hearts will be cluttered by fear and anxiety. We'll crumble when the phone call comes. We'll collapse under the pressure of work and life. Our knees will wobble and our spines will weaken with each difficulty.

But when we decide to recognize God as Creator and trust that He's in control of everything, a supernatural peace will flood into our hearts. And it will be exactly what we need to surrender every worry into His hands and rest in His goodness.

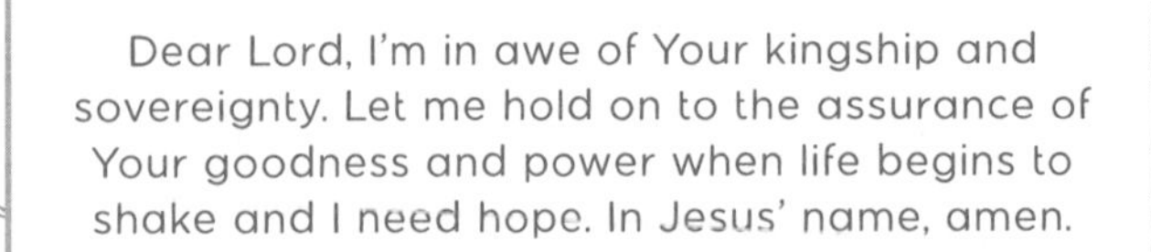
Dear Lord, I'm in awe of Your kingship and sovereignty. Let me hold on to the assurance of Your goodness and power when life begins to shake and I need hope. In Jesus' name, amen.

HIS INSTRUCTIONS

I advise you to obey only the Holy Spirit's instructions. He will tell you where to go and what to do, and then you won't always be doing the wrong things your evil nature wants you to. For we naturally love to do evil things that are just the opposite from the things that the Holy Spirit tells us to do; and the good things we want to do when the Spirit has his way with us are just the opposite of our natural desires. These two forces within us are constantly fighting each other to win control over us, and our wishes are never free from their pressures.

GALATIANS 5:16–17 TLB

There are a lot of voices out there telling us what to do. They fill us with ideas about how we should live and what's important. They often justify our natural desires, helping us rationalize our wants and wishes. And while at face value these desires may not seem wrong or harmful, we have to evaluate whether they truly align with God's will for us.

The question is this: Will we choose to obey the Lord, or will we satisfy our fleshly yearnings? If we're believers who love God and are committed to following His path, the choice is clear. Let's be women who seek the Holy Spirit's instructions above all else. Let's pray for the spiritual ears to hear His leading. And let's drop our wills and reach for His.

Dear Lord, I'm listening. In Jesus' name, amen.

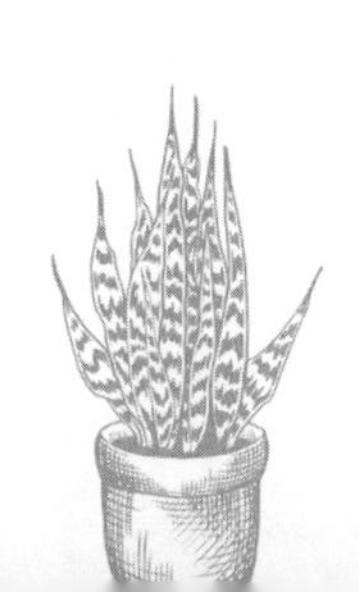

WHEN YOU DON'T KNOW WHAT TO DO

But anyone who needs wisdom should ask God, whose very nature is to give to everyone without a second thought, without keeping score. Wisdom will certainly be given to those who ask. Whoever asks shouldn't hesitate. They should ask in faith, without doubting. Whoever doubts is like the surf of the sea, tossed and turned by the wind.

JAMES 1:5–6 CEB

Have you ever been faced with a difficult situation and had no idea how to move forward? Have you been at a loss for ideas and solutions, uncertain of the right next step? Friend, this is a normal occurrence because we have limited knowledge. There's no way we'll have all the answers, and we weren't designed to either.

But God has all wisdom necessary for us to navigate every situation and circumstance rightly. Scripture encourages us to ask Him for this wisdom without hesitation and without doubt. Go straight to the throne of God and tell Him where you're needing discernment. Talk about your confusion with honesty and humility. Remember, it's in the Lord's nature to impart wisdom. He is never stingy and desires to meet our needs according to His will and timing.

He will fill you with understanding so you can do the right thing. God will clear out your uncertainty and replace it with clarity. Just ask.

Dear Lord, reveal Your truth to me and show me how to make choices that are good for me and glorify You. In Jesus' name, amen.

THE FRUIT OF BELIEVERS

But when the Holy Spirit controls our lives he will produce this kind of fruit in us: love, joy, peace, patience, kindness, goodness, faithfulness, gentleness and self-control; and here there is no conflict with Jewish laws. Those who belong to Christ have nailed their natural evil desires to his cross and crucified them there.

GALATIANS 5:22–24 TLB

The Holy Spirit's work in the heart of a believer is important because He helps grow and mature faith. The Spirit plays a key role in producing fruit that authenticates our faith. But first we must truly belong to Christ. His work begins when we say yes to a saving faith through Jesus. And once we do, ridding our lives of evil and selfish desires, the Spirit has room to produce godly qualities within us, like love, joy, peace, patience, kindness, goodness, faithfulness, gentleness, and self-control. Without His help, these fruits can't thrive.

Friend, have you secured your eternity? Is Jesus Christ your personal Savior? Are you giving the Holy Spirit freedom to transform you from the inside out? If not, there's no better time than now to surrender your life into His hands by accepting the gift of salvation through Jesus, God's one and only Son. He came to earth, died on the cross to pay for your sins, and rose from the grave three days later.

Dear Lord, I repent of my sins and surrender my life to be transformed through Jesus' sacrificial love and the Spirit's work. In Jesus' name, amen.

BLESSINGS FROM ENDURANCE

Blessed are those who endure when they are tested. When they pass the test, they will receive the crown of life that God has promised to those who love him. When someone is tempted, he shouldn't say that God is tempting him. God can't be tempted by evil, and God doesn't tempt anyone.

JAMES 1:12–13 GW

When a life storm hits, we often struggle to see the big picture. We become shortsighted, only able to focus on the dumpster fire. Maybe we panic. We might crumble into a million pieces. Or we check out emotionally because we can't handle the situation. Our hearts become full of doom and gloom.

But James reminds us that our willingness to stay engaged will be blessed. Perseverance will pay off. But first we need God to give us courage to stand strong. We need His divine perspective. We need His comfort and care. We need His strength. And we need to trust that God is fully aware of the details surrounding our testing, is fully able to get us through it, and is fully engaged in our well-being.

There is always purpose behind the trials we face. They're designed not to take us out or ruin our lives but to deepen our faith in ways only adversity can do. And they're always for our good and His glory.

Dear Lord, empower me to be strong and present when the trials come. In Jesus' name, amen.

PERFECTION IS NOT THE GOAL

Let everyone be sure that he is doing his very best, for then he will have the personal satisfaction of work well done and won't need to compare himself with someone else. Each of us must bear some faults and burdens of his own. For none of us is perfect!

GALATIANS 6:4–5 TLB

You see, friend, perfection is not the goal of the Christian life. Paul powerfully unpacks that truth in today's verses. The only perfect person ever to walk on planet Earth was Jesus, so let's not allow such an impossible pursuit to clutter our hearts a minute longer.

Instead, let's give ourselves a break, as well as those around us. Recognizing that most of us are doing our best, trying to navigate this crazy world and stay sane, will help to settle our anxious spirits that say we're not doing enough or not doing it good enough.

The reality is that we will fail and let others down. We'll fall into sin and climb our way back out again. But if we let God's love crowd out the condemnation that comes from not being perfect, a sweet acceptance of our human condition will prevail.

Dear Lord, thank You for permission and grace to be imperfect as I try to live in ways that please You and bless others. In Jesus' name, amen.

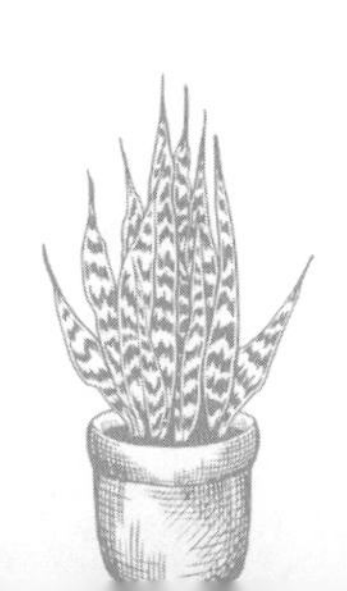

YOU HAVE PERMISSION

Avoid stupid controversies, genealogies, and fights about the Law, because they are useless and worthless. After a first and second warning, have nothing more to do with a person who causes conflict, because you know that someone like this is twisted and sinful—so they condemn themselves.

TITUS 3:9–11 CEB

The Bible tells us that, if it is possible, we're to live at peace with others. It tells us that peacemakers are blessed and urges us to turn the other cheek. We're told to love our enemies and bless those who curse us. We can deduce, then, that love and peace are important parts of the Christian life. Our hearts should be so full of them both that they spill out as we interact with those around us. But not everyone follows this command.

Today's scripture gives us permission to walk away from those who would rather bring chaos. We should kindly call them out once, then a second time, in hopes of calming the waters. If they persist in their grumbling remarks and fighting words, however, we can confidently declutter them from our lives. We don't need constant conflict littering our days.

Loving others doesn't mean we can't have healthy boundaries. We don't have to tolerate consistent and persistent bad behavior. Ask God to help you know when decisions need to be made.

Dear Lord, thank You for permission to walk away from toxic people. In Jesus' name, amen.

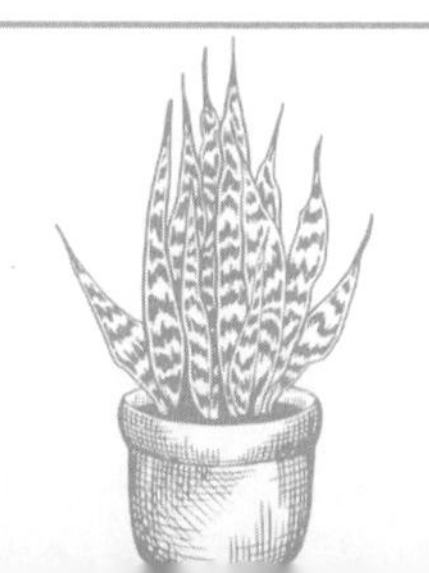

GOD WILL MAKE A WAY

Righteous people cry out. The Lord *hears and rescues them from all their troubles. The* Lord *is near to those whose hearts are humble. He saves those whose spirits are crushed. The righteous person has many troubles, but the* Lord *rescues him from all of them. The* Lord *guards all of his bones. Not one of them is broken.*

Psalm 34:17–20 GW

Friend, you're going to be okay. It may not seem so now, but God will make a way, just as He's done every time before. Go ahead and release every fear that's filling your heart as you let faith permeate the empty spaces.

Remember that the Lord is with you every step of the way, even when the diagnosis is scary, the loss is great, the divorce is complete, and the job is unnerving. He hears you cry out for help and will provide a rescue at the perfect time and in the perfect way. God is ever present, and He will save you from the crushing feelings that overwhelm.

Let's be aware that fear has a way of overtaking us quickly. Unless we release it into the heavenly Father's capable hands, this persistent and pervasive worry will become our operating system. It will wipe out our peace and stifle our joy. You are safe in the fullness of God's love.

Dear Lord, thank You for promising to make a way for me to navigate through every trouble. In Jesus' name, amen.

UNFAITHFUL

You are like an unfaithful wife who loves her husband's enemies.
Don't you realize that making friends with God's enemies—
the evil pleasures of this world—makes you an enemy of God?
I say it again, that if your aim is to enjoy the evil pleasure of
the unsaved world, you cannot also be a friend of God.

JAMES 4:4 TLB

The Bible often uses the metaphor of marital adultery to represent a believer's unfaithfulness toward God. As we read in the Word how deeply He loved His people, and as we recall all the times He has shown up powerfully for us, we can easily imagine the pain our disloyalty causes the Lord.

Every time we choose the world's values over His, we grieve Him. Rejecting God's ways for earthly ways means we're making friends with His enemies. James tells us we can't be in both camps. Our hearts are either full of the Lord or full of the world.

Does anything or anyone hold a more important place in your heart than God? If so, you're at risk of being His enemy. Put an end to those unfaithful ways and instead pursue a deeper relationship with Him. Let loyalty to the Lord characterize your days.

Dear Lord, forgive me for the times I've chosen the world's way of living over Your commands. Nothing the world offers will satisfy, at least not for long. Help me to chase hard after You alone. In Jesus' name, amen.

THE COMMAND TO LOVE

Love is patient; love is kind. Love isn't envious, doesn't boast, brag, or strut about. There's no arrogance in love; it's never rude, crude, or indecent—it's not self-absorbed. Love isn't easily upset. Love doesn't tally wrongs or celebrate injustice; but truth—yes, truth—is love's delight! Love puts up with anything and everything that comes along; it trusts, hopes, and endures no matter what.

1 CORINTHIANS 13:4–7 VOICE

This passage of scripture is powerful! While we'd like to be loved this way, walking out this kind of love toward others is surprisingly difficult. How can we be patient and put up with those around us when they're infuriating? How can we love without being jealous of someone whose life seems perfect? How can we have a servant's heart and not worry about our own needs being met? The answer? . . . God.

Ask the Lord to love others through you and then watch as He gives the compassion needed. He'll empower you with strength. He'll enable you to see others as He sees them. And as you trust in Him for this kind of love, it will saturate your heart, filling it up with mercy and grace to pour out on others. You'll be able to love from a place of divinely inspired affection.

Dear Lord, I trust You to remove anything in my heart that keeps me from being Your hands and feet in this world. Empower me to love well. In Jesus' name, amen.

HE WILL GIVE YOU WORDS

"Look, I'm sending you as sheep among wolves. Therefore, be wise as snakes and innocent as doves. Watch out for people—because they will hand you over to councils and they will beat you in their synagogues. . . . Whenever they hand you over, don't worry about how to speak or what you will say, because what you can say will be given to you at that moment. You aren't doing the talking, but the Spirit of my Father is doing the talking through you."

MATTHEW 10:16–17, 19–20 CEB

Imagine how much Jesus' words must have calmed the disciples, assuring them the Spirit would put words in their mouths when needed. They didn't have to stress over what to say. They didn't have to shy away from confrontation either, worried they'd say something wrong. This knowledge gave them freedom to do what they were called to do and allowed them to trust God to do what He promised to do.

If you're a believer, the Holy Spirit lives within you. Let Him remove your fear and fill you with the right words at the right time too. Release those anxious thoughts. Ditch the insecurities littering your heart. Ask for confidence to believe that God won't leave you to navigate difficult times alone. Your job is to be prayed up and scriptured up. . .and to choose to trust the Lord.

Dear Lord, I'm confident You'll give me words when I need them. In Jesus' name, amen.

SOWING AND REAPING

Make no mistake: God can't be mocked. What you give is what you get. What you sow, you harvest. Those who sow seeds into their flesh will only harvest destruction from their sinful nature. But those who sow seeds into the Spirit shall harvest everlasting life from the Spirit.

GALATIANS 6:7–8 VOICE

This is one of the most power-packed concepts in the Bible because we're able to see it play out in our own lives. We can influence how things turn out based on what we put in. What we give is what we get. Of course, God is in control, and the will of God will always be done. But, friend, have you seen the principle of sowing and reaping at work?

If you fill your life with righteousness and are mindful to follow the Lord's leading, your actions will yield goodness. The harvest you enjoy will reflect your faithfulness. But if you stockpile sinful thoughts and attitudes, fleshly desires and deeds, you will reap the natural consequences of disobedience. The harvest will reflect your destructive sinful nature.

Make this one and only life on planet Earth matter. Live for God with your words and actions and watch the blessings that will come from doing so. Nothing is sweeter than a life well lived for the glory of the Lord.

Dear Lord, help me to intentionally sow goodness into my life so I'm set up to reap blessings. In Jesus' name, amen.

THE TRUTH OF WHO YOU ARE

"Aren't two sparrows sold for a small coin? But not one of them will fall to the ground without your Father knowing about it already. Even the hairs of your head are all counted. Don't be afraid. You are worth more than many sparrows."

MATTHEW 10:29–31 CEB

Make no mistake that you're deeply loved by the one who created you, friend. God took His time thinking you up, planning all the details that make you special. It's not by chance that you look as you do or live where you live. The timing of your arrival onto the kingdom calendar was intentional. Your gifts and talents were given to you on purpose. God even planned who would make up your family and community. And, like today's scripture reminds us, He knows the exact number of hairs on your head.

Since the Lord has been so deliberate to create you and care for you every day, why is your heart still cluttered with insecurities? Why do you doubt your value? What keeps you from embracing the truth of your great worth in His eyes?

Today, talk to God about your fears and worries. Be honest about your hang-ups and insecurities. He is the only one who can replace them with the truth of who you are.

Dear Lord, this world beats me up and makes me feel worthless. I don't feel lovable or important. Please fill my heart with Your truth and comfort me. In Jesus' name, amen.

GUARD YOUR HEART

Above all else, watch over your heart; diligently guard it because from a sincere and pure heart come the good and noble things of life. Do away with any talk that twists and distorts the truth; have nothing to do with any verbal trickery. Keep your head up, your eyes straight ahead, and your focus fixed on what is in front of you. Take care you don't stray from the straight path, the way of truth, and you will safely reach the end of your road.

PROVERBS 4:23–26 VOICE

This passage of scripture starts with a command and then proceeds to tell us how to walk it out. We're given a road map, if you will, to follow. And as we do, it will guide us to live in ways that glorify God.

The admonition to guard our hearts is a call to action. It's not a passive suggestion in any way, nor is it a once-and-done event. Instead, it's an important rule for living because if we don't, the heart will quickly lead us astray. It can send us down wrong paths we're not prepared to navigate. But if we protect the purity of our words, keep our eyes from distractions, and stay focused on what is true and right, then our obedience will be blessed.

Dear Lord, please declutter my heart so I can fill it with good and right things as I guard it from the world's littering. Empower me to move forward with purpose. In Jesus' name, amen.

DO GOOD THINGS

May we never tire of doing what is good and right before our Lord because in His season we shall bring in a great harvest if we can just persist. So seize any opportunity the Lord gives you to do good things and be a blessing to everyone, especially those within our faithful family.

GALATIANS 6:9–10 VOICE

How can we be a blessing to others? When someone is hurting, we can be there to listen. If someone is in need, we can find ways to help. We can mow a lawn, cook a meal, offer a ride, or clean a home. We can sit with someone who is grieving or read a book to the elderly. If they need groceries, we can shop for them. We can even bless anonymously, not wanting to draw attention to ourselves. As believers, we should say yes to any opportunity we have to do good for others, even if it inconveniences us.

Be careful that you don't look away when someone needs help. Don't be so focused on yourself that you can't see the broken in front of you. And ask God to soften your heart to love others with great passion and purpose, especially other believers.

Let go of judgment or a critical spirit. Release any selfishness inside. You were created to do good things.

Dear Lord, fill my heart with the desire to do what is right and just in Your eyes and for Your people. In Jesus' name, amen.

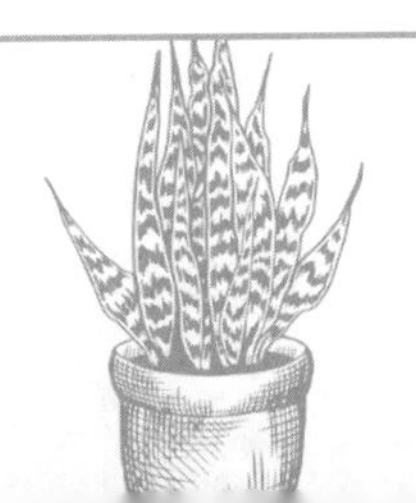

DEALING WITH SIN

Why is it that you see the dust in your brother's or sister's eye, but you can't see what is in your own eye? Don't ignore the wooden plank in your eye, while you criticize the speck of sawdust in your brother's eyelashes. That type of criticism and judgment is a sham! Remove the plank from your own eye, and then perhaps you will be able to see clearly how to help your brother flush out his sawdust.

MATTHEW 7:3–5 VOICE

We have all fallen short of the glory of God—every single one of us. We've all made rude comments to those we love, yelled at our kids in frustration, told lies to justify our behavior, gossiped behind someone's back, and made choices we knew didn't glorify the Lord. But instead of dealing with our own sin, we've been quick to point it out in others. We've judged them while overlooking our own shortcomings.

Rather than being full of criticism toward others, what if we focused on ourselves first? What if we focused on living righteously each day, repenting of the sin that so easily overtakes us, instead of pointing fingers?

God loves a humble, repentant heart, and He will use such a person to encourage and challenge a believer trapped in sin.

Dear Lord, remove my judgmental spirit and replace it with one of repentance and compassion. Let me deal with my own sin before I venture to help others. In Jesus' name, amen.

THE TRUTH IN LOVE

By speaking the truth with love, let's grow in every way into Christ, who is the head. The whole body grows from him, as it is joined and held together by all the supporting ligaments. The body makes itself grow in that it builds itself up with love as each one does its part.

EPHESIANS 4:15–16 CEB

For context, in the previous verses Paul was talking about maintaining unity in the body of believers since we all serve the same God. He was encouraging maturity of faith so we're not easily deceived. And so, recognizing these—unity and maturity—we are to speak the truth with love. Why? Because we're on this faith journey together.

The Lord delights in community, and He designed it to be an encouraging training ground to help each other live righteously. It's where we discuss God's goodness. It's where we support one another to walk out the callings placed on our lives. And it's where we call out someone who's headed down the wrong path. But. . .our motivation is deeply rooted in love. Truth and love go together.

It's because we love someone that we speak truth. And because we know the truth, we are called to love. As believers, we're constantly being transformed to be more like Christ, who is full of love and truth, which means we should be too.

Dear Lord, declutter my heart of selfish or critical motives, and let me be a thoughtful part of my community of fellow believers. In Jesus' name, amen.

HE CAN DO ALL THINGS

You bound the world together so that it would never fall apart. You clothed the earth with floods of waters covering up the mountains. You spoke, and at the sound of your shout the water collected into its vast ocean beds, and mountains rose and valleys sank to the levels you decreed. And then you set a boundary for the seas so that they would never again cover the earth.

Psalm 104:5–9 TLB

Because we know God is capable of securely putting the world together, speaking the waters and land into place, we can be confident in His help with our relationships. We can know the Lord will handle our financial frustrations and health-related worries. There's no doubt God can guide us through the struggles of parenting toddlers and teenagers. He can manage every fear and anxious thought that traps us. Our infertility challenges are safe in His hands. The Lord will meet us in our grief. There is nothing our magnificent God cannot or will not navigate with us.

Friend, let this understanding purge the doubt that keeps you from reaching out for His help. Let it remove whatever stops you from believing that He can do all things. God is with you. He's for you. He is able! So let Him grow your faith until your heart and head align with this life-changing truth.

Dear Lord, fill me with a deep understanding that You're always able and willing. In Jesus' name, amen.

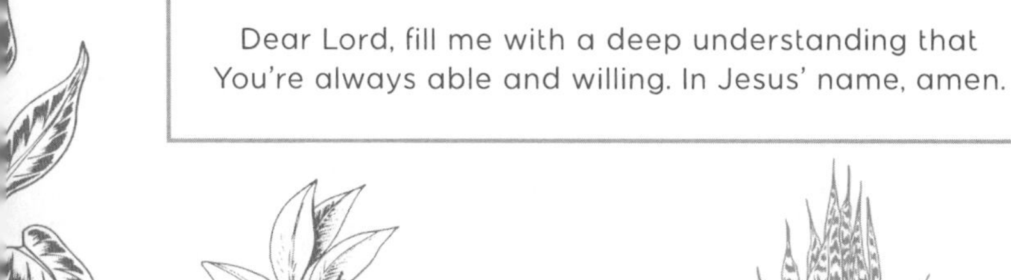

A FLOOD OF GENUINE LOVE

Stop being mean, bad-tempered, and angry. Quarreling, harsh words, and dislike of others should have no place in your lives. Instead, be kind to each other, tenderhearted, forgiving one another, just as God has forgiven you because you belong to Christ.

EPHESIANS 4:31–32 TLB

How can we be kind when we're angry all the time? How are we supposed to express tenderhearted care for others when we're always picking a fight? Are we known to be mean-spirited toward those we love? Do we use harsh words against someone who frustrates us? Is negativity cluttering our ability to love people? Good questions!

Scripture tells us to be compassionate and gracious with each other. We're to be gentle and sensitive. The Lord also reminds us of the forgiveness we have received through Him, which in turn should compel us to quickly forgive others. Don't miss this command, friend. It's important for righteous living that delights the Lord.

With God's help and our obedience, our hearts can change and genuine love can flood into the spaces where negativity used to dwell. The pessimism can be purged. And rather than feeling cynicism toward others, we can let the Lord turn our hard hearts into pliable ones.

Dear Lord, I repent of my anger and hard-heartedness. I'm sorry for the seasons of sinning when I lived with such disparagement. Give me a new heart filled with pure love and care for those You've put in my life. In Jesus' name, amen.

GOD'S LOVING CORRECTION

My son, do not ignore the Eternal's instruction or lose heart when He steps in to correct you; because the Eternal proves His love by caring enough to discipline you, just as a father does his child, his pride and joy.

PROVERBS 3:11–12 VOICE

One of the ways God shows His unwavering love to us is through correction. He cares enough to redirect our actions because He wants the very best for those who love Him. And when we—by accident or disobedience—take the wrong path, God will step in. Just as a good parent intervenes with love and care, so He does for us.

The problem is that many of us don't like to be called out. We don't appreciate being told we're in the wrong. And when we sense His displeasure, we tend to feel guilt or shame. But since there's no condemnation in Christ, we can know those unhealthy feelings come from the enemy. Whereas God gently and lovingly corrects us, Satan fills our hearts to the brim with condemnation.

Ask the Lord to show you the truth. Let Him replace any guilt and shame with a sense of value in His eyes. And allow the Father's love to settle in your heart, enabling you to trust His guidance through the ups and downs of life.

Dear Lord, thank You for taking a loving interest in my life and wanting only the best for me. In Jesus' name, amen.

TASTE OF HIS GOODNESS

Taste of His goodness; see how wonderful the Eternal truly is. Anyone who puts trust in Him will be blessed and comforted. Revere the Eternal, you His saints, for those who worship Him will possess everything important in life. Young lions may grow tired and hungry, but those intent on knowing the Eternal God will have everything they need.

PSALM 34:8–10 VOICE

This passage from Psalms is an invitation to experience the goodness of God in your life. You may have heard the powerful testimonies of others or seen Him work miracles in someone else's difficult circumstances, but have you personally tasted of His goodness? If not, what are you waiting for, friend?

As soon as you choose to trust Him to satisfy your needs, blessings will follow. Letting go of doubt or control will result in a filling of God's comfort. As you praise His name, seeking to know Him better and giving Him glory, you'll begin to experience a deeper sense of contentment that will be unmatched by anything the world can offer.

Let's declutter ourselves of earthly things and embrace eternal things instead. Let's taste and see that the Lord is good! And let's keep our eyes and hearts focused on our good and gracious God who meets every need, because that's how we'll find hope until we see Him face-to-face.

Dear Lord, I want to experience Your faith-building goodness so I can share it with those who need hope and encouragement. In Jesus' name, amen.

DON'T EVER TRUST YOURSELF

If you want favor with both God and man, and a reputation for good judgment and common sense, then trust the Lord completely; don't ever trust yourself. In everything you do, put God first, and he will direct you and crown your efforts with success.

PROVERBS 3:4–6 TLB

Sometimes we choose to fill our minds with our own wisdom. The reality is that we're smart women who have some years of experience under our belts. We also bloat our confidence with human strength at times, certain we can handle whatever comes our way. And all too often we reveal a lack of faith in God, deciding that our ways are best and trusting them above all else. Unsurprisingly, this usually ends badly.

The writer of the verses above offers a stark warning for believers, saying we shouldn't ever trust ourselves apart from God. Any tendency to lean on our own understanding is best released and replaced by a resolve to trust in the Lord alone. Such a resolve will help ensure that we follow His will and ways, finding success at His hand. And because God always gives us good judgment and common sense, our trust in Him will bring us favor with both Him and others. His name will be glorified through our obedience.

Dear Lord, help me to be mindful of the times I'm working in my own abilities rather than trusting in Yours alone. I don't want anything to obstruct Your goodness in my life. In Jesus' name, amen.

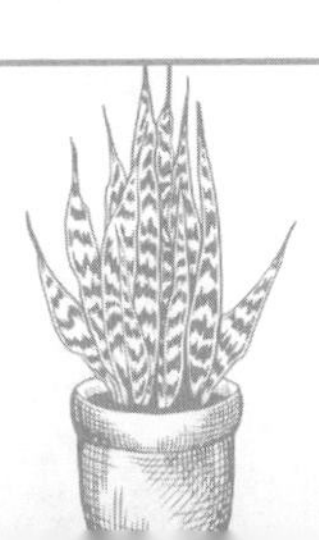

A HARVEST OF GOD'S APPROVAL

Wherever there is jealousy and rivalry, there is disorder and every kind of evil. However, the wisdom that comes from above is first of all pure. Then it is peaceful, gentle, obedient, filled with mercy and good deeds, impartial, and sincere. A harvest that has God's approval comes from the peace planted by peacemakers.

JAMES 3:16–18 GW

In these verses and throughout his writing, James focuses on comparing the life of an unsaved sinner or a fleshly, lukewarm follower with the life of a true believer committed to faithfulness. The first two can often exemplify characteristics that go against God's plan for living, including jealousy, rivalry, and every other kind of evil. These two groups of people don't please the Lord, and their actions leave a path strewn with heartbreak and brokenness.

But those who are genuine believers devoted to righteous living partake of a harvest that has God's approval. They worship Him in spirit and in truth as they walk in step with the Holy Spirit who dwells within them. And they are guided by wisdom that brings forth peace, gentleness, obedience, mercy, and every good thing.

Sow godly living into your life each day. Know what the Bible says about pleasing God through words and actions. And be quick to pray for help when you feel those fleshly desires begin to battle against what you know is true and right.

Dear Lord, help me to declutter my heart of worldly ways that bring You displeasure. In Jesus' name, amen.

PURSUE THESE TWO GOALS

Have two goals: wisdom—that is, knowing and doing right—and common sense. Don't let them slip away, for they fill you with living energy and bring you honor and respect. They keep you safe from defeat and disaster and from stumbling off the trail.

PROVERBS 3:21–23 TLB

If you take today's verses to heart and focus on these two goals—godly wisdom and common sense—there will be no room in your life for worldly clutter. But recognize, friend, that they're something you must cling to and nurture. They will require time to cultivate through the Word and in prayer. You'll have to be intentional to seek the Lord daily, especially when your default setting is jumping to your own conclusions.

When you pursue these goals wholeheartedly, though, God's wisdom and knowledge will give life to your weary spirit. You will feel energized to keep going by faith. You'll enjoy solid footing as the Lord directs your journey. You'll experience a steadiness to your soul that reflects your steadfast devotion to the Lord. And you will enjoy the goodness of God in significant and meaningful ways.

We're living in crazy times, with deception and evil everywhere. Be committed to keeping your eyes on the Lord and letting His leadership uncover the path that leads to victory. Seek His wisdom before each next step.

Dear Lord, let my only wisdom and common sense come from Your Word and the Holy Spirit's guidance. In Jesus' name, amen.

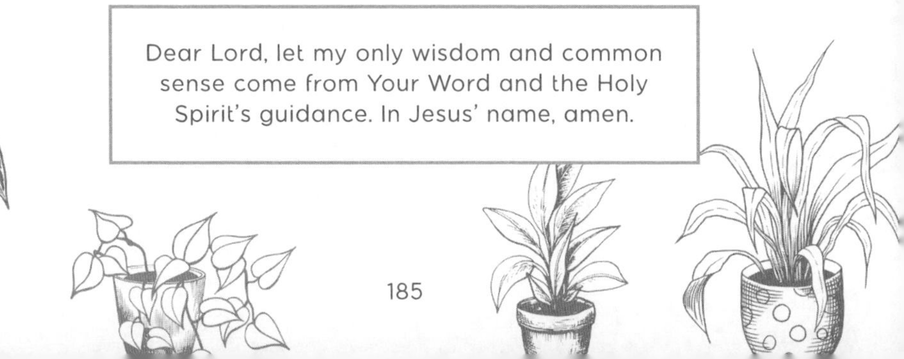

A ROYAL PRIESTHOOD

But you are not like that, for you have been chosen by God himself—you are priests of the King, you are holy and pure, you are God's very own—all this so that you may show to others how God called you out of the darkness into his wonderful light. Once you were less than nothing; now you are God's own. Once you knew very little of God's kindness; now your very lives have been changed by it.

1 PETER 2:9–10 TLB

In these verses, Peter was writing to believing Jews, using a series of Old Testament attributions they would recognize. He told them they were chosen by God, a royal priesthood, holy and pure, and God's very own; these were all things said of the nation of Israel. In this way Peter was affirming they were special to the Lord.

Peter may have written these words to Jewish believers, but we know that every believer—Jew and Gentile—is an important part of God's kingdom here on earth. Each one of us is a priest of sorts, proclaiming the Lord's kingship and praising His name.

Hold your chin up today, friend. You matter greatly to the Father, and He delights in your very existence. Purge every thought, every lie, that whispers anything different to you. Keep your heart filled with His truth and live knowing you're loved and valued.

Dear Lord, it does my heart good to know that I fit into Your kingdom and that I'm loved. In Jesus' name, amen.

THE GOODNESS OF GOD'S RULES

Blessed Lord, teach me your rules. I have recited your laws and rejoiced in them more than in riches. I will meditate upon them and give them my full respect. I will delight in them and not forget them.

PSALM 119:12–16 TLB

Some think following God's will and ways might weigh them down. God's rules feel restricting, causing them to worry they'll never have fun again. They think His commands will ruin their lives, no one will want to be their friend, and invitations to group gatherings will dry up. That kind of thinking needs to be decluttered.

The reality is the complete opposite. There is safety and blessing in obedience. It's where we find strength. Pressing into God is how we gain wisdom and discernment. Being mindful of His instruction is what ushers in comfort and washes us in peace. As believers, we're privileged to dig into the Word and learn how and why to live in ways that delight the Lord's heart.

Today, let the goodness of God's rules replace the lies saying they're unreasonable. Reject any stinkin' thinkin' that tries to tell you differently. And with passion backed by scripture, trust that His heart for you is always good, in every way.

Dear Lord, I confess I've misjudged the Word and considered it too restrictive in the past. Help me to remember that Your laws bring freedom and goodness, while the world can only offer me slavery to ungodly things. In Jesus' name, amen.

NOT ALLOWED

But no instrument forged against you will be allowed to hurt you, and no voice raised to condemn you will successfully prosecute you. It's that simple; this is how it will be for the servants of the Eternal; I will vindicate them.

ISAIAH 54:17 VOICE

While spoken by Isaiah, this verse is a promise from God about the restoration of the city of Jerusalem. He promised that no weapon made for their destruction would succeed. What a relief it must have been to hear these words and realize that the Lord was in charge.

This same promise is applied to believers today. Rest assured that no matter what chaos and calamity the enemy of our soul plans against us, it will fall flat because God is still in charge. Be it a nasty divorce, a misguided child, a dire diagnosis, identity theft, bankruptcy court, infertility or miscarriage, or the death of a loved one, He is still with us and always will be. His Word is our sword, faith is our shield, and His armor is our protection.

Let this truth swell to full capacity in your heart today. You can stand confidently, knowing the Lord will hold you steady and bring victory. He has already overcome the world! And regardless of what comes your way, the heavenly Father is right there with you, protecting you and guiding your every step.

Dear Lord, You won't allow any weapon forged against me to hurt me. You won't let any condemnation leveled against me to prosecute me. In Jesus' name, amen.

SCRIPTURE INDEX

OLD TESTAMENT

NEW TESTAMENT